the Art of
Tradition

A Christian Guide to Building a Family

by Mary Caswell Walsh
illustrations by Helen Caswell

Living the Good News, Inc.
a division of The Morehouse Publishing Group
Editorial Offices:
600 Grant Street, Suite 400
Denver, CO 80203

Cover Design and Layout: Val Price

Cover Photography: Val Price, Linda Sterrett

Printed in the United States of America.

ISBN 1-889108-34-0

for Matthew
companion, lover, healer, artist, father of our children

for Teresa and Elly,
children of light, women of character, generous-hearted,
truth-minded, radiant blessings

I thank God for you
my family

Acknowledgments

This book provided me with the opportunity to meet and talk to people of every race and culture about the traditions that enliven their families' lives together. I have had lengthy chats with moms and dads, ministers and teachers, young and old. Sometimes we spoke for a few minutes by phone, sometimes at length in a hospital room or at our kitchen tables. Always people have been gracious, open and eager to talk about their families, their spirituality and their traditions. I thank each of you. This book could not have been written without you.

I am especially grateful to Fr. John Boivin and his staff at the Office of Ethnic Ministries, Archdiocese of Chicago; Fr. Jim Garcia for input on Filipino traditions and Fr. Peter Hung for his insight on Vietnamese traditions. My special thanks to Richelle Romo, who shared Native American traditions; Micheline Steacy for her Chinese American traditions; Valerie Glowinski for her Polish resources; Isabel Zbaracki for her Mexican American songs and traditions; Rev. Clarence Kelly for insights into African American traditions; Victoria Rommel for sharing recipes and ideas; and Gia Xenakis Branit for Greek Orthodox traditions. My thanks to Fr. John Gambro, O.P., for Latin translations. I am grateful to the chaplains of West Suburban Hospital and Loyola Medical Center for helping me learn about the needs of those who are dying and mourning. My special thanks to Rev. Robert Long, Chaplain Ellen McBride, Deacon Cliff Dienberg, Chaplain Linda Bronersky and Fr. Jim Creighton, S.J. I am grateful to Christine Callan for her insights into single life, her friendship and ongoing support. I am grateful to my editors, especially Kathy Mulhern, for her support, hard work and great ideas.

My family has been my greatest support and I thank you from the bottom of my heart for your love, your good ideas, even your criticism. My thanks for the support of all our sisters and brothers, nieces and nephews, but especially Bob and Janetha, Phillip and Maria, Teresa and David, who have made suggestions and let me use recipes.

My husband, Matthew, challenged and refined my theology at times and had much to offer about music. He is an ongoing source of strength for me as together we continue to learn about marriage and parenting. Our daughter Teresa has been a constant reminder of the traditions that have been important in our family, and our discussions gave me insight into what our adolescents are struggling with. Our daughter Elly gave me considerable help in using our computer and transcribing and arranging the songs.

It is from my parents, Dwight and Helen, that I first learned to value Christian traditions. I am grateful for all they have taught me through the years. It has been a special joy to work with my mother on this book. Her illustrations, recipes and suggestions add so much, and the book has been a great excuse for lengthy long-distance phone conversations. Thank you both for your love and support.

Table of Contents

Foreword

When we worry about losing something valuable, we often seek to learn more about it in order to protect and preserve it. When we begin to feel a loss of vigor, we might read something about physical conditioning. If we are fearful that our investments might decline in value, we start reading financial magazines. If we fear that our own family might be heading for the endangered-species list, we turn to the advice columns of popular magazines or we read a good book about improving family life. Mary Walsh has written a *very good* book about exactly that: pumping more vitality into family life.

Each year, respected pollster Daniel Yankelovich and his associates survey the trends of contemporary America to determine what's bothering us as a people. They inquire about our common concerns and fears of the day. In recent years, the number one concern of Americans has been the same: the decline of the family.

We all agree that this concern relates to a variety of issues: the loss of family time in an overly scheduled life, the difficulty of maintaining strong and vital marriages when wife and husband are constantly pulled in different directions, the distractions of television and now the computer, the draining of any support for families outside their own almost private attempt to survive. Everyone agrees that it is a challenging time for families.

Yet there is good news too. We have recognized the nature of the enemy and many families want to overcome its damaging influence. We are coming to an agreement that families can face these erosive forces and not be passive to their incessant demands. Families can intentionally *be* family. They *can* spend more time together. They *can* communicate more honestly. They *can* let their care and love for each other show more clearly.

In other words, when we speak of the challenges of creating a rich family life, we are not dealing with the race of a tidal wave toward a defenseless coastline. Families have power and they are more willing these days to use that power. The life of the family is something that can be controlled and adjusted. It is not automatic that your family life or mine needs to become a casualty of the chaos of our times.

So what might we do? How about doing what we already do, but doing it a little better. The family doesn't need a list of extras. Its plate is already full.

Mary Walsh asserts, and I agree, that one of the best ways to ensure family cohesiveness and vitality is to incorporate meaningful rituals into the routine of family living. Surprisingly, this is not an impossible, or even a difficult, challenge. Humans have quite gracefully inserted rituals into the routines of daily living from the dawn of civilization. Unfortunately, during an epoch like our own, where we have suffered a loss in even basic *human* behavior, a loss of respect for each other, and perhaps even a loss of respect for ourselves, we lose the rituals of civility, the rituals that alert us to the deeper aspects of our lives.

Recently, we celebrated the life and death of Victor Frankl, the Austrian psychiatrist who survived the horrors of the Nazi concentration camps. In his classic book, *Man's Search for Meaning,* he argues that the key to a rich and hopeful life is to find meaning, especially meaning affecting the future, in one's current life. He observed that those who lost a sense of meaning and purpose often succumbed to the forces of diminishment and death.

Connecting daily events with rituals that imply "there is more going on here than meets the eye" seeds those events with human and spiritual depth. In fact, I like the language of the great Jesuit philosopher and scientist, Teilhard de Chardin, when he notes that we are not so much human beings seeking to be spiritual, but rather spiritual beings seeking to be human.

Nothing humanizes us more than engaging in meaningful rituals, especially when they are connected with those moments that can give us a sense of life's basic meaning and importance. And for most of us, these are family events beginning at birth and pouring forth at regular intervals all the way to the time of death.

When we lose a sense of ritual, we lose something of our spirit. When we regain it, we rediscover something deep within ourselves, the abiding presence of our God.

David Thomas
Graduate Professor of Community Leadership and Family Studies
Regis University, Denver, Colorado

Coauthor of the recently published *Our Families, Our Faith*

Introduction: Traditions for Living

The infant leaves the cramped comfort of the womb. The 6-year-old who once thought Daddy knew everything becomes a 16-year-old who thinks Daddy knows nothing. My grandmother grew up riding a horse, but my daughter wants to become an astronaut. In my day, unsafe sex meant risking pregnancy, not AIDS, and breaking our family rules might have meant taking a puff of a cigarette in the high school parking lot, not smoking crack in the grammar school bathroom.

As individuals, as families and as a society we experience transition when the world as we know it changes. Many of these changes are natural and predictable. We expect the birth of a child to have an effect on our marriage. We expect our children to grow up, leave home and create their own families. We expect our parents to grow older and eventually die. But even expected changes can prove unexpectedly difficult.

What enables us to deal with change in a creative, life-giving way? How do we create lasting marriages? How can we raise joyful, healthy children and launch them into the world without us feeling left behind? How do we live so that, at the end of life, we can face death with peace rather than despair? After twenty years of working as a psychotherapist, and more recently as a hospital chaplain, with individuals and families in crisis, I have concluded that those who can acknowledge and appreciate the past are best able to live with joy in the present and to move with confidence into the future. Tradition feeds the present with the wisdom and strength of the past.

To meet the challenges of life, we need to access the traditions that helped our parents and our parents' parents. We need access to the practical wisdom of the ages. Yet, because we face problems our ancestors never dreamed of, we will need to adapt ancient wisdom and interpret our heritage for the needs of the present. We must become builders of tradition, crafting vessels out of our life experience to carry us and our children and our children's children safely into the future.

We live in a society of instant information and instant gratification. We have come to expect instant coverage of world events and instant relief from our headaches. Odds and ends purchased forty years ago are sold in antique shops, and youth, rather than old age, is revered. Modern technology and scholarship have challenged our assumptions about our world and about ourselves. Tradition has been undervalued. Our societal rituals are frequently little more than marketing strategies; political policies may be influenced as much by polls as by principles; and religious tradition is often considered passé not only by agnostics and atheists, but by the keepers of the traditions themselves. We have more time-saving devices than any generation in history, but how many of us feel we have time for ourselves, for our family and friends, for a relationship with God? Constant change makes us fearful and insecure.

Some of us enthusiastically embrace change to the neglect of tradition and end up spiritually undernourished. Others of us, disillusioned by contemporary culture, attempt to return to the past, but resisting and refusing change can have equally damaging effects. An archeology professor I once had used to tell of a Peruvian community that lived on a mountain. They had such great reverence for the dead that they would bury the deceased and their belongings and, respectfully avoiding the graves and property of the dead, move up the mountain. After several generations of moving up the mountain, the people were running out of usable land. We need tradition, yes, but we need tradition that speaks to and emerges out of our lived experience.

Numerous traditions have nurtured Christian families throughout the centuries, traditions that have been enriched and individualized by ethnic, cultural and personal experience. Most of these exist in an oral tradition, passed on from parent to child. Unfortunately, these traditions are frequently lost, displaced or neglected precisely when families need them most, such as when life challenges their ethnic identity and family stability. Such stability must find its way through a plethora of social changes and destructive forces, including immigration, acculturation, poverty, homelessness, divorce, addiction, domestic violence, sexual abuse, rising crime rates, disease, famine and war.

Many young adults lack the guidance and support they need to develop strong, loving relationships or to create a meaningful and soul-satisfying single life. Many young couples, eager to build a healthy and spiritually rich family life, lack the tools to do so. Many families have lost the heritage and relationships that might have supported them. Other families have difficulty adapting old traditions to a new family structure. In single-parent homes or homes where both parents have jobs outside of the home, it can be difficult to come up with the energy to do anything more than get dinner on the table, do the dishes, tuck the kids in bed and switch on the television.

So many of the young couples I meet are discouraged or frightened. They fear that their love and faith will not be sufficient to keep their marriages alive and to give their children what they need. I have worked for many years with people in crisis; I have walked with people through their darkness, and others have walked with me through mine. Has living and working with crisis and suffering brought me despair or burnout? On the contrary, walking with people through their difficult times has made me a person of hope. I have witnessed again and again the resilience of humanity, the adaptability of love and the power of faith.

My experience has taught me that faith and love are more than enough when they are shared in intimate relationships, between generations and across great ancestral spans. Our spiritual heritage has great power to offer us, when it is used. Unfortunately, the rich traditions that can strengthen faith and love too often lie packed away in attics or forgotten on dusty shelves. We have what we need to flourish in all that life gives us, but we resign ourselves to survival. I believe it was the English novelist and spiritual writer C.S. Lewis who compared Christians to deep-sea divers encased in suits designed for many fathoms deep "marching bravely to pull out plugs in bathtubs." Doesn't this describe many of us?

How can we adapt the wisdom of the past to meet the needs of the present? I believe we do it as people have always done it, by entering into conversation with others, with our families and friends and neighbors, and with those who have gone before. Pope John XXIII spoke of us as the "latest link in a long and sacred chain."[1] This book is a conversation, a sharing of insight, experience, recipes, prayers, stories and rituals passed on from one link to the next in this sacred chain.

I imagine myself sitting at my kitchen table with a pot of coffee and a plate of muffins. I talk with my neighbor about her experience as a single mother; I talk with my own mother about what she did when she was newly married; I speak with my great-grandfather about how he courted my great-grandmother; I even speak with Mary about the songs she sang to Jesus to still his fears of the dark. This conversation has gone on for centuries, and will continue for centuries to come. Pour yourself a cup of coffee, or tea if you prefer, and pull up a chair. Join me at my kitchen table.

1

Sanctifying Solitude:
Two Halves Don't Make a Whole

"The sole cause of man's unhappiness is that he does not know
how to stay quietly in his room."—Blaise Pascal, *Pensées*

Most of us, when we think about Christian traditions for the home, think about
families. Many people put off practicing any kind of religious tradition in their
homes until they are married and the first child comes along. It may seem odd,
then, to embark on this journey with a chapter on single life, but that is where it
begins. Single people are the fundamental building blocks of all families and communities. A healthy society requires strong families; healthy families require strong
individuals. One of the most significant changes in American life is the increase
in the number of single people. In 1980, 23 percent of all households were single-
person households, three times as many as in 1970. By 1995, 25% of all households were people living alone. Many people wait longer to marry; some choose
not to marry; and many find themselves single later in life due to divorce or the
death of a spouse.[1]

Historically, singleness has been considered a time of limbo between childhood
and parenthood. Mythically, limbo is a place of oblivion where souls are barred
from heaven...it's not a good place to set up housekeeping! We need to redefine
single life as a time of growth and spiritual fulfillment.

I recall a young couple who came for marriage counseling. The romance, they said, had gone out of their marriage and the harder they tried to get it back, the worse their relationship became. When asked what they were doing for their marriage, they talked at some length about having breakfast, lunch and dinner together, grocery shopping together, doing the laundry together. Are you ever apart? I asked. Well, no. In fact, they were a little afraid of being alone.

Few marriages can withstand this much togetherness. These two had married, at least in part, out of a fear of being alone. Rather than giving them the warmth and security they craved, their togetherness was fast driving them crazy. Rather than using their time of single life to become people with something to give each other, they had spent their single years searching for another to make them whole. It doesn't work that way.

We need to nurture the capacity for singleness, for we cannot build healthy relationships if we don't know how to be alone with ourselves. In the words of psychologist Salvador Minuchin, "Human experience of identity has two elements: a sense of belonging and a sense of being separate."[2] If we experience only our separateness, we become isolated, lonely and selfish. But if we reject our separateness we become parasites, looking always to others to fulfill us, unable to give ourselves freely.

One woman, the wife of an alcoholic, told me how she had become so caught up in trying to control her husband's unpredictable behavior that she lost all sense of self. She had become so dependent on another that she had no life or identity of her own. She gave me the most concise definition of co-dependency I have ever heard: "A co-dependent is someone who, when they are about to die, sees someone else's life passing before their eyes."

Isolation and selfishness are spiritual symptoms that let us know when we need to grow, either in our capacity for solitude or our capacity for relationship. We need relationships to become a unique Self, and we need a Self to be able to have true relationship. As Jesus tells us, we are to love others as we love ourselves. Those who look outside of themselves, whether to a spouse or to their children or to a religious order, to give their lives meaning may find marriage, parenthood and religious vocation disappointing. At the same time, those who cannot share themselves with others, who refuse to learn and grow through interaction with others, will likely find life empty and unfulfilling.

Single Christians, whether single prior to marriage, after divorce or as a single vocation, need to discover God's presence in solitude. Author Susan Muto writes:

"Personally, as a Christian, I try to center my singleness in the heart of Jesus, the Single Word spoken by the Father. In the Word made flesh, I am at home with my single calling and united spiritually with all other people, contemplatively present to His will and actively serving the members of His kingdom."[3]

When singles live with this perspective, it no longer makes sense to wait until a child comes along to get an Advent wreath or say grace at meals. It will be every bit as important for a single person as it is for married people to bring to daily home life the practices that infuse ordinary life with the extraordinary significance of God's presence. Such practices may include simple things such as saying grace even when eating alone, saying one's rosary, engaging in spiritual reading, or making the effort to observe the holidays with friends. To neglect the traditions that nurture life on a daily basis is to starve our souls. For the purposes of this book, we will focus on single life as a period of growth preceding marriage, but it is important to remember that some of us will return to single life after marriage and some of us will live out our lives as single people.

Traditions of Self-Discovery

In the words of the Jewish mystics, we ascend to God by descending into ourselves. We seek God in the depths of our own hearts. One of the simplest and oldest traditions of self-discovery is the journal. There are as many ways to keep a journal as there are people. I suspect my mother, an artist, fills her journal with sketches. My own journal began 27 years ago, at the request of my spiritual director, and is filled with dreams and meditations. One person's journal might focus on concerns about the politics of the day and another's on the seasonal progress of a garden. The journal is an opportunity for reflection, a chance to immerse oneself in the moment. It gives us the time and place to take a second look at the events, people, thoughts and emotions that have filled our days.

When working on a journal, don't make rules for yourself that you know you'll break. Don't promise yourself that you'll write an hour a day before breakfast. Approach this commitment with some time thinking about your days, or your weeks, and asking yourself this: At what time of day, in what room or chair or part of the garden do I find myself wanting to sit still and daydream? Then give yourself that space you already crave. A mere ten minutes a day can reap unexpected treasures.

One of the most helpful exercises I know for getting in touch with one's deeper self is a breathing meditation of Eastern origin that I learned many years ago from Anthony de Mello. Breath has long been associated with God in the Judeo-

Christian tradition. The oldest word for *soul* in the Hebrew scriptures is *neshama*, literally breath.

Breathing in God

Sitting comfortably in a quiet place, close your eyes and focus your attention on your breathing. Breathe deeply, slowly, rhythmically for a few minutes. Imagine that the very air you breathe is filled with God's presence; each time you breathe in, you are filling your lungs with God's power and presence. Imagine yourself to be breathing out impurities and negative feelings and breathing in "God's life-giving Spirit."[4]

Whereas the journal helps us to reflect on ourselves and our life, this breathing meditation helps us to experience a deeper sense of self and, in the opening of our lungs, to take in life-sustaining air, to experience a greater sense of God's love-sustaining presence.

When we think of self-discovery, we tend to focus on the mind. However, those who have experienced significant pain, illness or grief will know that at times the mind cannot be counted on. At such times it helps to understand that we pray and relate to God and to others not only through our mind but also through our body. Religious people have often distrusted the body, seeing it as a source of temptation, but the scriptures describe the body as the temple of the Spirit. It is a holy place, a place where God comes to be at home with us.

I remember a client I had years ago, a lovely woman who was feeling very stuck. Her life was good, but a bit dull. There wasn't anything really wrong, except that she just wasn't happy. When I asked her if there was anything she had always wanted to do but hadn't, I expected her to talk about a trip she had longed to take, or a career she had wanted to pursue, or a relationship she missed. Instead, without a moment's thought, she told me that, yes, there was something she'd always wanted to do. She'd always wanted to roll down a hill. Why hadn't she? Well, she'd felt embarrassed. It seemed silly to her, and it probably seems silly to you, too. But a few weeks later she found a deserted hillside and let herself roll. It was a turning point in her therapy. Why? She had learned to listen only to her mind, but it was her body that could give her joy. When she began to listen to her body she began to enjoy her life.

Pay attention to what your body needs. Try different ways of letting your body approach God. Prayer is very different when standing or kneeling or walking or dancing or lying prostrate. Explore what happens when you approach God in physically different ways. What does your body have to tell you about yourself? about God?

Traditions of Remembering

I once took a group of adolescents, all in the early stages of recovery from addiction, on a pre-dawn hike up California's Mount Tamalpais, a sacred mountain in Native American tradition. The young people brought objects that they had selected to represent themselves. We hiked to the top of the mountain in darkness and waited for dawn. We sat there together and yet alone in the darkness and silence, wrapped in our woolly sweaters and private thoughts.

How long it took the sun to rise! I remember thinking, Just my luck, the one day I organize a hike, and the sun doesn't come up! Such impatience! But it did come up, slowly, silently, a glow of pink and then a bright beginning of gold and at last a clear cloudless day. We buried our "self" symbols on the mountain, one by one sharing our stories with one another. One young woman buried a lock of her hair, cut off in childhood, and shared with us her disappointments and her dreams. Six months later, at a celebration of her first year of sobriety, she told me that whenever she felt like abusing she would look up at the mountain and tell herself, "The real me is at the top of that mountain," and she would stay sober another day. This ritual, rooted in Native American spirituality, connected our personal reality with the greater reality of mountain and dawn. The awareness of the greater reality helped this young woman to face the daily challenges and temptations of her life.

Tradition helps us to remember, and in remembering to discover who we are in the bigger picture of life. When Jesus at the Passover Seder told his disciples to remember him in the breaking of the bread, he called to mind the unleavened bread of the exodus from Egypt and the manna in the wilderness. He created a new ritual from the ingredients of ancient rituals.

We need to remember. And we need not only community rituals, but also personal and familial rituals of remembering. Many of us need go no further than our attics or our scrapbooks to recognize our need to stay in touch with our past. After the terrible Oakland Hills fires, people talked a lot about what they chose to take with them when time for choosing was brief. Some took their pets, family photos, a musical instrument or an heirloom. Two young girls, to the delight and amazement of their conductor, chose to take their San Francisco Girl's Chorus music folders.

What we choose to hold on to at such a moment tells us something about who we are, what we value and who we want to become.

What object would you choose? What does that tell you about yourself? We can learn much about ourselves by reflecting on the experiences we choose to remember and the objects we choose to keep. We become builders of tradition when we take the stuff of our daily lives and through reflection, uncover and reveal their deeper meanings. Ordinary objects can have symbolic power and carry extraordinary meanings. To get a sense of this, try this meditation on a familiar object.

Meditation on the Ordinary

Begin by choosing an object that is part of your daily life, something that appeals to you or speaks to you in a special way. Get to know your object. Set it on your desk, kitchen table or bedside table where you will see it often. Take a few minutes every day to reflect on what this object says to you about who you are. Is it different when you feel it with closed eyes? Does it have a smell? Does it bring up memories? Is it associated with an event or experience that was important to you?

Once you have uncovered the meaning this object has for you, find a way of giving it a place in your life, or a way of celebrating the meaning it has revealed. For example, you might carry the object in your pocket, or place it on the mantel on special days. Like my young friend, you might take a mountain hike and bury it on the mountain. Or you might give it to someone you love with the story it holds for you.

I once meditated on a piece of obsidian that I had picked up on a hike to Sunshine Shelter, a camp at the base of the Three Sisters mountains in Oregon where my father and brothers and I used to go mountain climbing. The stone was smooth on one side and rough on the other. It came from the depths of the earth and had once been hot and liquid, but through volcanic crisis had gained solidity and strength. When I looked into it I saw that it was a mirror. It brought back memories of the smell of penuche my father made over the campfire, the feeling of numbness in my toes and the bite of the cold air on my cheeks, the beauty of the mountain meadows bright with lupin and Indian paintbrush, the glittering creek and the water ouzels winging their way upstream.

What did this little stone tell me about myself? It spoke to me of the strength that my own molten experiences of crisis had given me, how my own experience of pain had taught me to see more deeply into the pain of others, as if their pain were reflected in the depths of my own. It reminded me of people I love and moments I treasure. And it made me hungry for my father's penuche. In this simple way, I found God in a little black rock. Where is God in these thoughts and memories? God is in the hope that pain has meaning. God is in the beauty of creation. God is in the love I have for my family. And God is in my father's relentless optimism (who else would try to make penuche over a campfire?).

I keep my little stone in a bowl in the corner of my bedroom where I pray. I have added other objects over the years: locks of my daughters' hair, a pine cone from the spot where my husband proposed, a green stone from Jerusalem, a small clay figure made by my sister-in-law before her death. Occasionally I will hold one of these objects in my hands when I pray, revisiting and allowing myself to be nurtured by the memories it inspired. They remind me of what I need to remember, or want to remember, about my life. They have helped me *discover* who I am, and help me to *remember* who I am.

What relationships, events and experiences do you need to remember? What simple ways can you discover to remember them? One friend writes thank-you notes on her birthday to certain people who were important in her growth (a teacher, a friend who stood by her through a difficult time). You may want to revisit a place where you had a meaningful experience or observe the anniversary of a special day.

I believe that if we ever really see anything, we will see God, for the creation bears the indelible mark of the Creator. But how often do we really look at anything, be it an object, an experience or even a relationship? We take so much for granted...how often do we look with the curious, penetrating gaze of a child? And having seen, even in a brief glimpse, something sacred, how do we keep that memory alive, to nurture us on those days when we cannot see?

Traditions of Daily Transition

Whatever our calling, in our personal lives and within our relationships we can expect to face change. Through the centuries, Christians have found ways to celebrate the daily, personal experience of change, particularly the change of seasons and the changes of day from dawn to noonday to dusk to nightfall. By embracing these simple transitions, we prepare ourselves for the greater changes of life.

Taking a pre-dawn hike and enjoying a sunrise, or an evening stroll at dusk, can be a time to reflect on how change is an intrinsic and necessary part of our world, a time to be at peace in God's presence. Scripture gives us many words and ways to greet the movement of the day:

Prayer to Welcome Morning

It is good to give thanks to the Lord, to sing praises to your name, O Most High; to declare your steadfast love in the morning, and your faithfulness by night, to the music of the lute and the harp, to the melody of the lyre. For you, O Lord, have made me glad by your work; at the works of your hands I sing for joy. How great are your works, O Lord! Your thoughts are very deep!

(Psalm 92:1-5)

Prayer to Greet Evening

You have made the moon to mark the seasons; the sun knows its time for setting. You make darkness, and it is night....I will sing to the Lord as long as I live; I will sing praise to my God while I have being. May my meditation be pleasing to him, for I rejoice in the Lord....Bless the Lord, O my soul.

(Psalm 104:19-20, 33-35)

One of the oldest and best-known of Christian traditions is the observance of the hours. In the early Church, individual Christians devoted themselves to prayer at fixed times. At first, dawn and dusk were observed, but gradually other hours were also observed. The Liturgy of the Hours, or Divine Office, is the prayer of the Church and can be prayed individually or with others. It consecrates to God the whole cycle of the day and night and unites each individual Christian in prayer to the entire Church. (An abridged version is available, *Christian Prayer: The Liturgy of the Hours* [New York: Catholic Book Publishing Co., 1976].)

Traditions of Solitude

To find meaning and joy in single life requires nurturing both one's capacity for solitude and one's capacity for relationship. Only by owning our singleness do we develop integrity and learn to stand our ground with others. I do not know how we can become such persons without periods of solitude and times of reflection.

Each of us, introverts and extroverts, must make time for solitude. In this sense, singleness has less to do with our marital state than it does with the reality of the soul. We never stop being single—whole, unique, individual, alone with God—whether or not we get married.

What helps us grow in solitude varies from person to person. When my mother needs time for personal reflection or prayer, she goes off into the orchard with her sketch book. My husband listens to music. My father took long hot baths. I dig in the garden and periodically make trips to a Benedictine Abbey. One of my daughters bakes bread, and the other writes poetry. Many of us need silence, but some relax better with music; some of us need the outdoors and the immediacy of nature while others prefer the stillness of a chapel or a comfortable chair by the fire. Part of getting to know ourselves will involve experimenting with solitude and discovering our personal path to solitude. Prayer, personal reflection, spiritual reading, making use of devotional traditions and sacramentals can all be ways of discovering ourselves in God, and uncovering God within ourselves. (For an excellent resource on the ancient tradition of spiritual reading, consult Michael Casey's *Sacred Reading* [Liguori, MO: Liguori/Triumph, 1996].)

Sacramentals are signs, symbols, prayers, rituals and objects taken from ordinary life that become sacred in their use. Candles are a sacramental particularly appropriate to times of solitude. For nine centuries it has been traditional on the Feast of the Presentation, forty days after Christmas, to bless candles. Recalling the words of Simeon, who recognized in Jesus the "light for revelation to the Gentiles and for glory to your people Israel" (Luke 2:32), candles are blessed at the liturgy and brought home for use. These candles may be lit during meals, at times of prayer or on special occasions. The following prayer can be said when lighting the candle:

Prayer of Blessing

Jesus Christ is the light of the world,
 a light no darkness can overpower.
Blessed is God
 now and forever, Amen.

Votive lights (from the Latin word *votum*, which means "vow") symbolize seeking a favor from God, Mary or a saint, and making a promise. Vigil lights (from the Latin word *vigilia*, which means "waiting") are lit when making a petition to God and awaiting God's response, or they may simply symbolize your intention to wait on God, to be present to God. The lighting of vigil candles is sometimes accompanied by an invocation. Invocations are short prayers that can be repeated over and over.

Invocation Prayer

To find an invocation that will be especially meaningful for you, become quiet, search your heart and ask yourself what you most desire of God. Do you desire peace? Then you might pray, Grant me your peace. Do you feel lonely? Then you might want to pray, God be with me. Repeat this simple prayer over and over again, quietly and slowly, letting it lead you into a receptive stillness.

Suggestions:

God be with me.

Jesus, I love you.

Thanks be to God.

Your will be done.

Lord, have mercy.

Come, Lord Jesus.

Mary, mother of God, pray for us.

Alleluia.

I have a single friend who keeps candles about her home, lighting them each evening in remembrance of friends who are in her thoughts and prayers. Through the simple sacramental of these vigil lights, she not only fills the solitude of her home with love for others but she links herself to a sacred chain of tradition going back to ancient times: to the Jews who burned light in the temple sanctuary, at the Passover Seder and the weekly Sabbath meal; to the early Christians who burned oil lamps in their homes and house-churches; and to countless Christians who, throughout the centuries, have accompanied their prayers with the lighting of candles.

Holy water is another popular sacramental. People may take home some of the holy water blessed during the Easter Vigil to use in blessing themselves, others or objects. Some people keep a small font or receptacle beside their front door or bedroom door and bless themselves when they enter or leave their home. Blessing oneself in this way is a reminder of one's baptism, of one's new life in Christ.

Blessing of Holy Water

Simply place your finger in the water, make the sign of the cross and say, "In the name of the Father and of the Son and of the Holy Spirit, Amen." Other simple prayers that recall God's work in your life are also effective.

For example:
May Almighty God, the Father of our Lord Jesus Christ, who has given us a new birth by water and the Holy Spirit, and bestowed upon us the forgiveness of sins, keep us in eternal life by his grace, in Christ Jesus our Lord. Amen.[5]

Traditions of Relationship

To nurture our capacity for relationship, we need opportunities for faith sharing, and we will usually have to create them ourselves. Certainly we do this through the liturgy of the Church, but creating such opportunities also has a vital place in our homes and daily lives. One of my single friends said that she got tired of spending Christmas in the homes of her married friends (where she sometimes felt like a fifth wheel) and, one year, decided to invite a number of other single people to celebrate the occasion together. It was such a rewarding experience that they began to celebrate a number of holidays together. As she explained it, "I needed to create a family for myself."

Traditions of relationship also include acts of charity, reaching out to those in need. Self—with all its desires and obsessions and pleasures—can become all-consuming for anyone. Married people simply must take into consideration the other's needs, and parents turn themselves inside out serving their young children. Single people without children, however, need to seek out opportunities for service if they are to live healthy, fulfilling lives. Such acts of service need not be more dramatic or intense for single people than for married people, but they may need to be more intentional.

One single woman observes the tradition of tithing, giving a tenth of what she earns to those in need. I have another friend who always keeps an empty bowl on his desk to remind him of the hungry of the world. Every night he empties his pockets of change into this bowl, to be given to those in need. Through this simple personal tradition he brings into his solitude a constant awareness of the needs of others.

As important as it is to give money and material goods, we must also give ourselves. What do you have to give? Are you a gardener? One man helped neighborhood kids transform a vacant lot into a summer garden. Are you a handyman? Perhaps there is an elderly person who would welcome help with household repairs or yardwork. Do you like to read? Become a tutor or read to the elderly. If you like kids, offer to baby-sit for a single mom. Call your church or a service organization you believe in and ask them if they need volunteers.

Prayer for an Act of Service

For your strength does not depend on numbers, nor your might on the powerful. But you are the God of the lowly, helper of the oppressed, upholder of the weak, protector of the forsaken, savior of those without hope. Please, please...Lord of heaven and earth, Creator of the waters, King of all your creation, hear my prayer!

(Judith 9:11-12)

The best traditions are simple traditions. They find their strength in basic human emotions, desires and needs. Not surprisingly, such traditions, particularly relational ones, often involve food. Certain holidays, certain seasons, certain times of day are memorable because of the tastes and aromas that accompany them. One of the easiest ways to start a new tradition is to cook something good at a meaningful time.

Single people often deny themselves the joys of edible traditions because it seems a bother to cook for oneself. One of my favorite memories of my single days is of spending my birthday making Amish Friendship Bread for my friends. I remember sitting at the kitchen table in my little basement apartment, drinking coffee and listening to music while I waited for the bread to rise. My friends would come over later in the day with dinner and we would sit down to hot bread with honey. They would go home with starter dough to make their own bread. Now I usually give my friends their starters in sturdy plastic resealable bags. Sometimes I tie the bag with a ribbon to which I attach a small card with these words: *May there always be bread on your table and God in your heart.*

Amish Friendship Bread

Make a starter by combining:

  1 package dry yeast

  2 $\frac{1}{2}$ cups warm water

  2 teaspoons honey

  2 $\frac{1}{2}$ cups flour

Stir starter daily (or put in a resealable plastic bag and squish it daily). Let starter ferment for 5 days before using. Starter can be kept indefinitely in the refrigerator. One-half cup of starter will make 2 loaves of bread. Reserve $\frac{1}{2}$ cup of starter and divide remainder into plastic bags for friends ($\frac{1}{2}$ cup each).

When ready to make bread, combine:

  4 cups flour

  $\frac{1}{2}$ cup starter dough

  3 $\frac{3}{4}$ cups lukewarm water

Mix well, adding water gradually. Cover and let sit overnight. In the morning, replenish your starter by taking $\frac{1}{2}$ cup of the dough that has sat overnight. Place it in the refrigerator for the next time. To the remaining dough, add (folding in):

  $\frac{1}{2}$ cup oil

  1 teaspoon salt

Gradually add 5 cups flour. Knead on floured board 5 minutes, adding flour as needed. Separate into two sections and put in oiled bread pans. Allow to rise 2 hours. Preheat oven to 425 degrees. Bake 20 minutes, then turn the heat down to 375 degrees and bake for another 1–1 $\frac{1}{4}$ hours or until loaf makes a hollow sound when tapped.

Another wonderful and adaptable tradition that brings together good food and friendship is a modern-day version of the old folk tale of stone soup. One of my mother's friends had a delightful "stone soup" experience while she was camping in Russia. As she cooked a pot of soup, a woman camping near her came over. This woman spoke no English, and my mother's friend spoke no Russian, but they could both speak soup. The woman brought over something to add to the soup. Then another woman came with something for the soup, and then another. It turned into a party, a wonderful meal and a true sharing in friendship although no one could understand the other's language. Try having a Stone Soup gathering. The following recipe is a basic stock that can be cooked ahead. Invite friends to come over, bringing a little something to add to the pot.

Stone Soup Stock

Wash 5-6 pounds of chicken (whole roasting chicken or chicken pieces). Place in a large kettle and add enough water to cover (about 3 quarts). Then chop the following and saute them together in butter:

> 2 onions
>
> 2 celery stalks
>
> 2 large carrots

Add the vegetables to the chicken and season with:

> 3 sprigs parsley, thyme and
>
>   oregano
>
> salt and pepper to taste
>
> $1/2$ teaspoon poultry seasoning

Also add 2 cups white beans (for "stones") that have been soaked overnight. (Discard the soaking water.) Bring to a boil and simmer for 2 hours. Skim off any scum on the surface, cut the chicken off the bones, and return it to the soup. You may refrigerate the soup at this point and reheat before your friends arrive.

Invite your friends to add their ingredients, which could include vegetables or herbs (finely chopped so they will cook more quickly), rice noodles or pasta (uncooked), chopped meat (cooked), sherry ($1/2$ cup is plenty), a squirt of lemon juice, or grated Parmesan cheese (just before serving).

Your friends may have stories to tell about the ingredients they have chosen, so indulge in storytelling as you add to the pot. One of my friends brought angel hair pasta because he is tall and thin. Another brought sliced carrots because she is learning to see in times of spiritual darkness. Another brought garlic to represent her strong Italian heritage.

Bring the soup to a boil, then reduce the heat and simmer another hour.

By developing our capacity for solitude, we develop our capacity for relationship. The ability to be alone before God is profoundly connected to the capacity to be fully present to others. Martin Buber states that in one's relationship with God, "you cannot make yourself understood with others concerning it, you are alone with it. But it teaches you to meet others, and to hold your ground when you meet them." He declares, and I agree, that "all real living is meeting."[6]

2

From Dating to Courtship: Friendship to Intimacy

One cannot say too much about tradition without consulting history. I found the history of courtship and marriage fascinating. There are so many rich, peculiar, wonderful, meaningful and silly traditions! We don't use the word "courtship" much anymore, and the word "dating" covers a wide range of experiences. Dating may refer to a shared social engagement with an acquaintance, a companionable evening with a close friend or an intimate sharing of self with a possible spouse. I suspect that the poverty of our vocabulary reflects the ambiguity and confusion we experience when we try to define and describe our relationships in a society that lacks clear boundaries, expectations and well-defined roles.

The difference between dating and courting is sometimes unclear in today's world. Webster's Dictionary defines a date as "a social engagement between two persons." Sharing a concert, sporting event, movie or dance for the sake of companionship and mutual enjoyment can greatly enrich our lives. By definition, dating is social, not private, and the level of intimacy appropriate to dating is that which is appropriate in the company of others. Traditionally, the inescapable presence of chaperones helped couples maintain the boundary between private and social. This boundary enables us to know who we are with each other.

I can enjoy a social engagement with a date; but if I reveal my more private self I presume a kind of friendship that involves a greater level of commitment than dating. If our friendship develops in such a way that we begin to contemplate sharing our whole selves and our whole lives, then we are courting. This kind of full sharing must be honest and must integrate the social, physical, emotional and intellectual aspects of our persons. The person who is physically intimate but emotionally distant, or emotionally intimate but spiritually distant, is going to have an unbalanced relationship. He or she is likely to hurt and be hurt by others.

It can be difficult for contemporary couples to respect each other's privacy when no social traditions exist to help them maintain the boundary between the private and the social. Today we are able to date not only without others being present, but without seeing our date, without knowing his or her family, without knowing his or her real name. Internet dating gives a couple the opportunity for immediate intimate communication without social risk, in the privacy of their homes. The Internet provides a wonderfully convenient, inexpensive form of communication, but it can also lend a false sense of privacy and encourage premature intimacy.

One young man was upset because his fiancée was having an affair with another man in the chat room of their computer program. She had discussed intimate thoughts, feelings, even sexual fantasies, but because she had never physically met this man, she felt she had not been unfaithful to her fiancé. At best, this is an excuse for dishonest behavior. At worst, it is a symptom of personal disintegration.

Our culture promotes premature intimacy, a sharing on a deep sexual and emotional level before commitment, often even before friendship. Like a young tree that never grew adequate roots, these relationships are likely to topple in the first strong wind, inflicting pain and causing damage. The Christian tradition of saving one's most intimate sexual self for the person you will vow to share your whole self and whole life with is not so uncommon as the media would lead us to believe. It is a tradition that makes a lot of sense both on a spiritual and psychological level.

I recall the young woman who came to me and, with considerable embarrassment, admitted that she was still a virgin. She seemed to think this was a problem. How is it a problem? I asked. She was afraid there was something wrong with her. Why? Because she was all of 17 years old and had never had sex. Today's young people have a societal image of instant relationships, promoted by the media onslaught of one-night romances. Youth have less supervision, fewer guidelines and face decisions about sex and intimacy at an early age. This can make dating difficult.

If you feel confused about what is "right" for you, ask yourself: Am I comfortable with what I am doing? Is my behavior, upon reflection, an honest expression of what I feel for this person? Do I feel respected and respectful? Am I being socially responsible? Am I feeling peace and joy or regrets and misgivings? When dating relationships are social, not private and rooted in honesty and respect, they are a wonderful opportunity for companionship.

Beyond Dating

There was a time when spouse selection involved such primitive methods as the capture or purchase of a bride. Those days seem far distant to us today (thank goodness). Less distant is the practice of having marriages arranged by the parents of the bride and groom, a custom still prevalent in many parts of the world. A Korean college classmate once told me how excited she was to be going home to meet (for the first time) a man her parents had selected for her. It was an approach to marriage that I found hard to imagine and yet, I confess I have some-times wondered if it might work better for some of us. Certainly one would bring to these marriages different and perhaps more realistic expectations. On the other hand, when I think of the men my parents might have picked... I'm glad I got to make my own choice! The evolution of marriage is an evolution from capture to purchase to negotiation to choice, but many of our traditions date back to the values of earlier times.

In my grandmother's day, you were likely to marry someone you had known from childhood. Young people began participating in social activities together as teenagers. The limited mobility of teenagers prior to the car helped to keep them under parental surveillance during courtship. The relative stability of neighbor-hoods and a less mobile lifestyle meant that couples had opportunities to develop relationships over an extended period of time. An old Scottish saying asserts that you should marry a person who lives close enough that you can see the smoke from his or her chimney. This saying reflects the belief that shared values and experiences make for a more cohesive relationship. Since World War II, society has become more mobile. Families move across country; young people go to another state for college or work; and the likelihood that you will marry the girl or boy next door is slim. This means that today's couples will have less time to get to know each other, and will probably share fewer lifetime experiences than their parents or grandparents did.

At the beginning of the 19th century, Americans were wary of romantic love as a foundation for marriage, associating it with immaturity and self-indulgence, but by mid-century, love was considered central to marriage.[1] There were, however, still significant differences in the perspective of marriage. Though people married for love, their marriage was a uniting, not just of individuals, but of extended families. Marriage had an acknowledged impact, not just on the individuals getting married, but on the whole fabric of society. As our culture has moved from the agrarian society of my grandmother's day to a more mobile industrial and urban society, the extended family has come to play a less central role. Today, marriage has become almost entirely a personal, private affair.

Instead of measuring intimacy by long familiarity with families, life stories and personal habits, today we often measure intimacy by sexual experience. Strong community life created natural, lasting relationships; many people today grow up in shallow communities, which lend themselves to superficial relationships. In the 19th century, when a couple became engaged the gentleman would "announce" their engagement by sitting in his future bride's pew at church rather than in his own.[2] Today we may not even know the people sitting in the pew next to us.

Some traditions have remained relatively unchanged. In the 19th century, the man presented the woman with an engagement ring. By the end of the century, formal announcements became customary. The engaged couple busied themselves with such activities as finding a home, purchasing furnishings and kitchen utensils, linens and the bride's trousseau.[3] Male and female roles were clearly defined.

Today's couple still acknowledges their engagement with a ring and announcements, and may busy themselves with the consumer aspects of homemaking, but their roles are far from clearly defined. Prior to, or during engagement, they must negotiate issues of premarital sex, cohabitation and marital roles without clear societal norms. You can no longer assume that the attractive man you met at the library is looking for a heterosexual rather than a homosexual relationship, or that the engaging young woman you were introduced to at the party last night wants to have children. Concerns about over-population, an improvement in the status of women and birth control have made it possible to value marriage without valuing reproduction and procreation. These changes provide today's couple with more choices and opportunities, but also with significant challenges and real temptations.

More critically, it's not just a question of figuring out what the other person wants. Often we don't know what we want for ourselves. Do I want to focus on career or child rearing, or both? And just how do I go about it? What do I need from my spouse? Why would marriage be "right" for me? Cheryl Mercer aptly describes contemporary courtship as "a labyrinth with hundreds of dead ends."[4]

Traditions of Courtship

One couple came to me for counseling because they were unsure whether or not to get married. They had been courting for several years and would go along quite happily for a while and then, for no reason apparent to themselves, enter into conflicts they were unable to resolve. Their happy times were characterized by periods in which they functioned independently, each absorbed in their own profession, with times together for shared entertainment. The periods of conflict were characterized by an initial disagreement (for example, whether to have Thanksgiving dinner together or with one or the other's family) that quickly disintegrated into a standoff and icy silence.

In fact, both their happy times and their unhappy times were much alike. Although they shared entertaining experiences, at neither time did they really talk to each other about their needs, their dreams, their insecurities or their faith. To discover whether or not they wanted a long-term commitment, they needed to begin by setting aside time to spend together just talking. In my experience, couples who have difficulty dealing with conflict also have difficulty in other areas of their relationship that only become apparent at the time of conflict. The most essential component of building strong relationships is honest and respectful listening and talking. Few of us, however, are born good communicators. Most of us have to practice, and that's what many of the traditions of courtship are all about.

At the same time that we have lost relational depth, our society has discarded the traditions that can help us measure where we are in a relationship and what each person might expect regarding commitment, childbearing and marital roles. The traditions of courtship help relationships develop and provide markers for the couple and for society. They help the couple know what level of commitment they have made to each other and what degree of intimacy they have developed.

Every age has had its issues. In early America, small, poorly heated homes provided little opportunity for privacy and little chance for young couples to converse intimately. To address this need, the tradition of bundling, when couples spent the night together in bed, fully dressed, became popular. It is not so difficult to find time to be private today, but much in our culture discourages the intimate conversation so necessary to developing relationship. The societal pressure to hurry into sexual activity can plunge people into pseudo-intimacy, that is, into a relationship in which physical intimacy is not accompanied by emotional and intellectual intimacy. The disparity inherent in pseudo-intimacy can create considerable stress on the individuals and on their relationship.

Much contemporary dating activity revolves around types of entertainment, such as movies and videos, which provide little opportunity for discussion. I have known couples who have dated for years without getting to know their partners' political or religious views, parenting philosophy or personal dreams. How is this possible? So much of their time together was spent being entertained that they did little to really get to know each other. This may be dating, but it is hardly courtship, and it does not provide people with a solid foundation for marriage.

Courting couples need to learn how to enjoy each other's company without distractions, to take time for an evening walk together or a leisurely dinner. They also need to learn how to argue constructively. Couples who come to me for counseling frequently don't know how to disagree in a positive, constructive way. They either never fight or fight in a way that aims to annihilate one or both partners. I once heard it said that when two people in a relationship never disagree, one of the two is unnecessary! If, in our relationships, we never experience disagreement or controversy, something is wrong.

One young couple struggling with this issue came to see me. The woman complained that she wanted greater intimacy in her relationship. Together the couple worked on sharing their feelings and beliefs in greater depth. A few weeks later she came in quite upset after their first argument. This had been a genuine disagreement in which both had expressed their conflicting desires, hashed it out and reached a compromise. Both agreed that they had reached a resolution, but the young woman was upset because it had been such an uncomfortable and difficult experience. I reminded her that she wanted greater intimacy in her relationship. Yes, she agreed. I pointed out that she had gotten just what she wanted.

True intimacy inevitably involves conflict. If one or both partners feel destroyed by conflict, or if the conflict is constant or abusive, get some counseling. Happily, communication problems are among the easiest of problems to treat. As a therapist, I have more concern for couples who don't communicate enough to know they have disagreements than for those who, through communication, unearth their differences. Because our society no longer provides ready-made traditions for this, couples need to create their own traditions of dialogue.

It helps to have an environment conducive to sharing; that is, you have to be able to hear each other. A nightclub or dance setting with loud music doesn't lend itself to good conversation. Make sure that you regularly spend time in places where it is easy to talk—a quiet coffeehouse or restaurant, or a beautiful natural setting such as a garden, park or country path. For those who find it difficult to talk, an activity that inspires discussion can help. One couple took up birding.

Armed with binoculars and Audubon books, they explored out-of-the-way paths in a local reserve. When conversation lagged, they could discuss beak color and habitat. Two young lawyers got into the habit of attending controversial lectures together, after which they would retire to a local coffeehouse and argue about the lecture over their cafe lattes.

My husband and I, in our courting days, would buy a loaf of French bread and some deli meat and cheese and take long rides into the California wine country. These weekly expeditions gave us leisurely opportunities to converse. My parents also went on picnics into the countryside. My mother has enormous talent when it comes to packing a picnic lunch. One of these picnics became so famous within the family because of the excellence of her spice cake that, fifty years later, our family still calls out "spice cake corner" every time we drive past the site of that picnic.

My parents' picnic dates started a tradition that evolved into a long-lived marriage (more than fifty years), five children and, to date, eleven grandchildren. Good atmosphere, good food and good company make for good traditions and wonderful memories. Here are some of my mother's recipes for a memorable picnic of your own. I include both the original recipe (because, if you have the time, it really is the best) and my own quick version.

Picnic Menu

Meat Pies
Fresh Fruit Bowl
Mom's Spice Cake

Meat Pies

Original recipe meat filling:
The best meat pies are made from leftover roast pork. For dinner the night before, we cook a roast large enough to provide ample leftovers. (Allow at least 1 pound per person.) Season the roast with sugar, ginger and soy sauce and bake, covered in a heavy kettle, at 350 degrees until done. (Meat thermometer should register 190 degrees.)

To make gravy, remove the roast from pan, pour liquid into a cup, spoon off all but 4 tablespoons of the fat and set the roasting pan on the stove on low heat. Use a wooden spoon to loosen bits of pork that have stuck to the bottom of the pan. Add 1/4 teaspoon sugar and 1/4 cup flour, and stir well. Slowly add 1 1/2 cups of liquid (pan juice plus water or beef broth if needed), stirring constantly. Bring to a boil, then lower heat and stir until thickened (about 5 minutes). Season to taste with salt and pepper. (If gravy gets lumpy, put it through a sieve.) Then the next day make the meat pie filling by heating 2 tablespoons butter and 1 tablespoon vegetable oil in a heavy skillet. Sauté together:

>   1 shallot, thinly sliced
>   4 baby carrots, thinly sliced
>   4 mushrooms, thinly sliced
>   1 can whole white potatoes,
>   drained and sliced

Add:

>   2 pounds leftover roast pork,
>   chopped
>   1–2 cups of gravy (to desired
>   consistency)

Quick version meat filling:
If you can't roast a pork the night before your picnic, make the meat pie filling using the same recipe but substituting this meat mixture for the leftover roast pork and gravy:

Brown 2 pounds of thinly sliced boneless pork butt in oil until done and remove from skillet. Make gravy by melting 2 tablespoons butter in skillet and add 1 tablespoon flour, stirring thoroughly. Slowly add 1 cup beef bouillon, stirring until thick.

Crust:

>   3 cups flour
>   1 $1/2$ teaspoon salt
> $1/2$ cup vegetable shortening
> $1/2$ cup chilled butter
>   approximately 5 tablespoons
>   cold water

Sift flour and salt together. Cut in shortening and butter, blending with fingers. Sprinkle in water, adding more if needed. Flour board and roll dough thin. Cut into 4-inch circles. Place meat filling in center of each circle. Moisten edge of pastry, fold closed and crimp the edges. Place the pies on a cookie sheet, prick the tops with a fork and brush with milk. Bake at 375 degrees until done (approximately 30 minutes).

Fresh Fruit Bowl

Add to bowl (with lid),

>   1 orange, peeled and separated
>   into segments
>   1 apple, chopped and sprinkled
>   with lemon juice
>   1 peach, peeled, chopped and
>   sprinkled with lemon juice
>   1 cup seedless grapes (halved)
>   or berries

Sprinkle lightly with sugar and stir. Then sprinkle on top $1/2$ cup shelled, chopped pecans and 1 tablespoon coconut.

Mom's Spice Cake

Mix dry ingredients together in bowl and set aside:

    2 $1/2$ cups cake flour (or regular flour)

    3 $1/2$ teaspoons baking powder

    1 teaspoon salt

    $1/2$ teaspoon cinnamon

    $1/4$ teaspoon nutmeg

    $1/4$ teaspoon allspice

Then cream together in a separate bowl:

    $3/4$ cup shortening

    1 $2/3$ cup brown sugar

    1 teaspoon vanilla

Add 3 eggs and blend. Then add dry ingredients alternately with 3/4 cup milk, beating well between each addition. Grease and flour two round pans and pour batter into pans. Bake at 375 degrees for 25 minutes (until cake springs back when touched in center). Let cool before frosting.

Butter Cream Frosting

Cream together:

    $1/2$ cup butter

    $1/8$ teaspoon salt

Gradually blend in:

    3 $1/2$ cups sifted confectioner's sugar

    2 egg yolks

    1 teaspoon grated lemon rind

    milk, enough to make spreading consistency (approximately 2 tablespoons)

Another couple created a tradition in the years of their courtship that they carried into their married life. They took turns selecting a book, and then they would each read the book and get together to talk about it. They shared a love of literature and would often select favorite novels; but each one could pick books that reflected that person's interests or beliefs.

When my husband and I were courting, he gave me an anthology of jokes to read. The book had been such a favorite in his family since the days of his parents' courtship that allusions to jokes in the book had become an integral part of his family's vocabulary. They have, over the years, become a part of our vocabulary as well.

In one of the cartoons, a man is greeted at the door to his home by his wife. The man is accompanied by an odd assortment of tiny people. The man is saying to his startled wife, "Just say hello, I'll explain later." We have made numerous references to this joke through the years, like the time he came into the bedroom holding a whole dead chicken by the neck. "Just say hello," he said, holding the limp chicken aloft, "I'll explain later." (It turned out the chicken was the gift of a local farmer on the occasion of our daughter's birth.) Reading the joke book introduced me to a very personal and enjoyable part of my husband's upbringing.

I know another couple who read their favorite childhood stories to each other, such delightful stories as Winnie the Pooh tales, *The Little Engine that Could* and Dr. Seuss stories. This kind of simple sharing readily inspires personal conversation.

Another tradition, which has lost favor in our electronic age, is the love letter. This is a tradition worth reviving (or perhaps updating by using the Internet). Many people feel free to say things in writing that they wouldn't dare speak aloud. More thought can go into a letter composed in private. Often a person inept at conversation is quite adept at written communication. Most of us have a tendency to take more care when our words have the potential of being preserved.

Examining Your Relationship

What kinds of questions do courting couples need to explore? What issues do they need to be aware of? Some questions come to mind:

- Do we share beliefs and values on issues central to marriage?
- Is either of us jealous, possessive or overly dependent?
- Can we talk about sex, politics, money or religion and feel respected and heard?
- Do we ever disagree? When we disagree, does one of us always give in?
- Do we both want children and share values on child rearing? (Offer to babysit a friend's child together and find out.)
- Are we in agreement about the roles we will play?
- Do we expect to share or divide housekeeping responsibilities and money management?
- Do we both want careers?
- Can we get along with each other's families?
- Are we both willing to make a commitment to sexual fidelity?
- Does either of us have alcohol or drug problems?
- Is either of us afraid of sex or afraid of commitment?
- Do we laugh at the same jokes?
- Do I like who I am when I'm with you?

No one will be comfortable with every issue, and no couple will agree on every issue. What matters is the willingness to take the time to talk, to have the courage to talk about pertinent, sometimes uncomfortable issues and to respect one another in the process. Traditions of dialogue are of particular importance when couples come from diverse religious or cultural backgrounds. Too often couples avoid areas of possible disagreement until children come along and the couple must decide in which tradition, or which combination of traditions, the children will be reared.

Gift-giving is another tradition of courtship that can symbolize the regard each person has for the other. Early in a relationship, couples enjoy such traditional gifts as flowers and candy. As the relationship becomes deeper and more intimate, the gifts can become more personal and individualized. One couple exchanged family trees. Another gave each other massages using scented oil. One of my favorite gifts from my husband (who is not into crafts) was a rosary he made out of purple beads and little wooden crosses.

St. Valentine's Day, celebrated on February 14, is popular among courting couples in the United States. It is unclear how St. Valentine, a priest and martyr, became associated with young lovers. The association apparently arose from the old notion that birds choose their mates on February 14th, St. Valentine's feast day. Red, traditionally the color of martyrdom in the Christian church, suggests the self-sacrificing nature of love, and friends and lovers exchange decorative cards, candies and tokens of affection. In the Middle Ages, many people wore love knots, symbols of infinity. These pins were often made of gold, a precious metal that never tarnishes.[5] Evelyn Birge Vitz, in her lovely book *A Continual Feast,* gives a wonderful recipe for edible "love knots." When I think of Valentine's Day, I think of my grandmother's heart-shaped sugar cookies that I make for my own sweetheart. These cookies, thin and buttery, are supposed to keep well, but I've never been able to test this.

Nan's Sweetheart Cookies

Cream together:
    1 cup butter
    1 cup sugar

Beat and add to creamed mixture:
    2 eggs

1 tablespoon water
1 teaspoon vanilla extract

Sift together:
    1 teaspoon baking powder
    $\frac{1}{2}$ cup flour

Add dry mixture to creamed mixture, beating lightly. Add enough flour to make a soft dough (about 2 cups) and turn onto floured baking board. Knead lightly and roll thin. Cut with floured heart-shaped cutter, place on cookie sheets and bake at 375 degrees for approximately 10 minutes.

Everyday rituals, simple recurring habits, can take on special significance, giving our lives greater security and richness. These rituals can be as uncomplicated as having breakfast together every Sunday morning, celebrating events important to the two of you (birthdays, job promotions, holidays, the anniversary of your first kiss), sending thank-you notes when your partner has been especially supportive or bunches of daisies when your partner has had a hard day.

Sometimes traditions evolve naturally and sometimes we need to make an effort. Often one partner develops traditions more easily than the other, but it should never rest entirely on one person. Don't be afraid to experiment, and don't worry if an attempt to enrich your relationship with personal rituals doesn't "work" immediately. Traditions, by their nature, evolve and grow, taking on deeper meanings over time. A bunch of daisies after a hard day is a nice surprise, but when your partner makes a habit (a tradition) of giving you daisies when you are going through a difficult time, then the flowers come to mean something more. You will, after a period of time, only need to see a vase of daisies to be reminded of your lover's ongoing support. Traditions don't need overt religious connotations to be spiritually nurturing. Any tradition that deepens and supports your love for one another and your appreciation and awareness of the goodness within each of you, is essentially spiritual and love-affirming.

Engagement Rituals

One of the most ancient symbols of union is the holding of hands. In some cultures, couples were not allowed to hold hands until they were betrothed. Couples naturally hold hands when sharing intimate sentiments. In Scotland, a couple's joining of hands is called "handfasting." In Ireland, the claddagh symbol, two hands holding a crowned heart, symbolizes the joining of two lives and is seen on rings and brooches that lovers wear. I know one couple who, after marriage, made a habit of simply holding hands each morning for a moment before beginning their day. It was a simple and profound way for them to express and recall their daily commitment to each other.

Although courtship has changed in many ways, the giving of rings continues to be a favorite tradition at the time of engagement. Like many traditions, it has been updated and adapted to fit the beliefs and values of society. Rings had different symbolic meanings at different times in history. When obtaining a wife was a business transaction and liquid assets were kept in the form of jewelry, engagement rings were associated with the purchase of the bride, and thus with the bride's subservient position. Yet as early as the time of the Egyptian pharaohs, silver and gold rings symbolized an eternal and indissoluble commitment, a meaning contemporary couples can appreciate.[6]

One Swedish custom calls for a woman to wear three rings: one for engagement, one for marriage and one for motherhood. In Italy, engagement and wedding rings were two bands of gold joined together. From the time of the 14th century, engagement rings were often inscribed with such loving sentiments as "To me til Death, as dear as Breath" or simply "This and my heart."[7]

Announcing the engagement to one's family is an exciting moment. I'll never forget the reaction of my future mother-in-law. Because I stood in such awe of her, I was infinitely relieved when she jumped up and clapped her hands, exclaiming, "I knew it! He's got a good one!" A little later, as we stood chatting in the kitchen, she took off the jet necklace and earrings she was wearing and, clasping the necklace around my neck, told me that it had belonged to my future husband's great-grandmother. What a wonderful moment. I do not have a son, so I can't give these jewels to his fiancée, but I shall certainly look for a similar gesture to help my daughters' future spouses feel welcomed into our family.

The announcement to my family was also memorable. I called my oldest brother and asked him to get the entire family assembled (no easy task when you have a large family). Of course he insisted I tell him why and I, never one to keep such things secret, readily told him. He, with an air of mystery, asked my mother to bake a cake, frost it and write on it H.G.M.Y.K. Perhaps she had an intuition, for she made her famous spice cake. When we arrived and told the family our news, there was considerable excitement, followed by puzzlement. H.G.M.Y.K.? My brother explained that the letters stood for "Happy Getting Married You Kids." Will I write these letters on the cakes I bake for my daughters' engagement parties? Probably. Will one be a spice cake? Of course! This is how family traditions are born. To give my daughters' fiancés a family heirloom or to decorate their engagement cakes with H.G.M.Y.K. celebrates both past and present and acknowledges their profound link. Family traditions remind us of the jokes, the joys and sometimes, the sorrows of the past that, when recalled, enrich our present.

It is traditional to throw a party to announce and to celebrate one's engagement. Customarily the bride's family hosts the party, but nowadays any friend or family member might do so. In Holland, the betrothal was an elaborate occasion, and special sweets called "bridal sugar" and a spiced wine called "bride's tears" were served. For my engagement party, my mother made *haggis*, a traditional Scottish dish that is considered a poor man's meal and is associated with the Scottish insistence on equality. "For rank is but the guinea's stamp, a man's a man for a' that," says the Scottish bard. The clan chief recited Robbie Burns's toast to the haggis. It was a grand and dramatic moment. Of course my mother cheated. Haggis is traditionally made of ground liver, sheep's heart, beef suet, onions, oatmeal and stock, cooked a goodly time in a sheep's bladder. Mom cooked it in a plastic oven bag (tantamount to heresy) but only because the local butcher wouldn't believe she was serious when she asked for a sheep's bladder.

Even if you aren't profoundly involved in or knowledgeable about your roots, bringing in ethnic traditions can add a great deal to your celebration. For one thing, most of the traditions that endure have done so because they are fun. I have included some ethnic traditions, but if you don't find one here that suits you, research your heritage at the library, or better yet, with the older members of your family who may remember these traditions.

A lovely Greek tradition involves making a kind of bread sculpture to celebrate an engagement. It can be served at the engagement party (or the wedding reception, if you prefer) or dried, varnished and saved. Perhaps you would like to make a small one to save for your future kitchen and a large one for the party. A ring is made of sweet bread and decorated with flowers and appropriate symbols. The bride and groom pull the ring apart to see who will have the upper hand in their marriage (presumably whoever ends up with the larger piece). This amusing tradition also carries a message: Just as bread sustains life, so humor, in the inevitable power struggles of marriage, sustains love. The beauty of these traditions is that they communicate such simple and necessary truths with few words and a liberal seasoning of fun. Our friend used this recipe for our wedding bread.

Annie's Wedding Bread

Combine in large bowl, stirring well to blend:

    2 cups all-purpose flour

    2 packages dry yeast (undissolved)

    1 tablespoon salt

Then add:

    $1/4$ cup honey

    3 tablespoons softened margarine or olive oil

    1 tablespoon grated lemon peel

    2 $1/4$ cups hot water

Beat well (2 minutes at medium speed on an electric beater). Then add 1 cup whole wheat flour. Beat until thick and elastic (1 minute at high speed). Stir in another cup of whole wheat flour gradually, and then add just enough flour to make dough leave sides of bowl (1 $\frac{1}{2}$ to 2 cups). Turn onto floured board and knead 10 minutes until smooth. Cover with waxed paper and a towel, and place in a warm place to rise for about 20 minutes.

Punch down. Reserve a fistful for decorations, and a small ball for a keepsake ring (if desired). Roll remaining dough into a long rope (about half the thickness you desire for your final ring). Form a ring, pressing ends together. Place ring on greased cookie sheet.

To make decorations, either make small shapes (as you would with clay) or press dough out with hands (or roll out with rolling pin) onto well-floured board and cut out desired shapes with cookie cutters. Make shapes smaller than you want them as the bread will rise and the shapes expand.

Traditional symbols include rings (symbol of union), birds, flowers, and grapes and vines, but you might personalize by using symbols especially meaningful to you, such as a music note for a musician, a hammer for a carpenter, a paintbrush for an artist, a stethoscope for a doctor, etc.

"Glue" decorations to the ring with beaten egg white. Brush bread with melted butter or olive oil. Cover loosely with plastic and refrigerate for 2–48 hours.

Preheat oven to 400 degrees. Remove bread from refrigerator and let stand 10 minutes (puncture any surface bubbles with oiled toothpick). Bake 30–40 minutes on lower rack. The bread is done when it sounds hollow when you thump the top. Brush with olive oil or melted butter. (For a glossy look, brush with egg white beaten with a little water and brushed on before baking.) The Keepsake loaf should not be oiled. It can be air-dried and varnished.

Choosing to marry someone is much, much more than breads and rings and flowers and romance. You will probably never make a more critical decision in your entire life. Your choice of a life partner will affect your future in ways you cannot possibly foresee. Spouses impact our careers, make their mark on our personalities, change our friendships and generally shape our lives in many new, unpredictable ways. The old phrase from the traditional wedding ceremony, "Marriage is not to be entered into lightly," is truer than we might understand. Of all decisions, this one demands wisdom.

On the other hand, few decisions in life can bring so much happiness. The traditions of courtship and engagement give us both opportunities to consider this decision with a spirit of discernment and ways to express our joy.

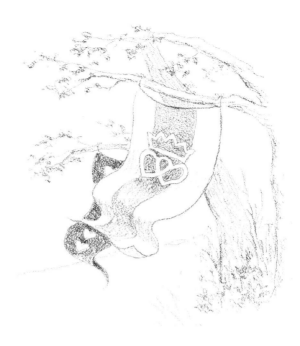

3

Matrimony and Marriage: One Plus One Equals One

For most of us, birth, marriage and death are *the* great events in our lives, so it is not surprising that there are more traditions connected with these life events than with any other. Many of these traditions, which had their origin in primitive human fears, attempted to ward off evil or promote good luck. A great number of ancient traditions may survive because, besides being customary and enjoyable, they tickle a trace of superstition in many of us.

What is the difference between superstition and spirituality? Superstitions usually involve a magical effort to control the world of the spirit. We send away the bad spirits and invite the good spirits through rituals that are thought to have power. Spirituality, in the Judeo-Christian tradition, involves not attempts to control God, but attempts to enter into relationship with a God who has first chosen us in love. We seek not to control God, but to do God's will.

Many superstitions are rooted in the fear of arbitrary and malicious powers. The Judeo-Christian tradition is rooted in our belief that God loves us and cares for us. In human practice, the line between superstition and religious observance is often a thin one. In fact, if we were to eliminate all traditions that had their origin in human superstition, we would have little left. What began as superstition can evolve into an expression of faith, and what began as an act of faith can disintegrate into mere superstition. The heart of the matter revolves around the issue of control and our image of God. Do I believe in a malicious and arbitrary God whom I can manipulate? Or do I trust in a loving God, seeking to do God's will?

Many wedding traditions that arise out of superstition do not really reflect our current beliefs. I include a number of these traditions, however, because they can add much to the joy of the wedding celebration and because they provide us with a link to our past (which I believe is always a part of us), but to use them means translating them to fit our belief in a God who has chosen us in love to live in relationship. Sometimes we will need to adapt and alter old traditions to fit our current beliefs and sometimes we will need to become creators of traditions that will more fully reflect what we have come to know about ourselves and our God.

If we use traditions to help us experience the underlying meanings of our life events, we must have an idea of what we believe. Some of us will have relatively clear ideas about what marriage means to us, gleaned from whatever religious teachings and social attitudes we have grown up with, as well as from the image of marriage we have acquired by observing the marriages of family and friends. Many of us will have less clear, sometimes confusing and even contradictory ideas about marriage. We will have witnessed unhappy and unsuccessful marriages and fear a similar fate.

Christian teachings on marriage and sexuality that might guide us have often been confusing, paradoxical and ambiguous. In fact, sexuality and marriage have frequently been devalued in Christian history. Although the apostle Paul took the Jewish view that sex was a part of God's creation and therefore good, he valued celibacy over marriage because he expected Christ's imminent return. St. Augustine, whose teachings continue to strongly influence the thinking of our own time, described marriage as good in the begetting of children, the mutual love and faithfulness of the spouses, and in its sacramental nature; and yet Augustine, while teaching the goodness of marriage, simultaneously reflected a pessimism born of his own preconversion experience.[1] Before he was married, Martin Luther called marriage "a hospital for incurables" and "a necessary evil" though it was also "God's work and commandment."[2] He underwent a dramatic change of viewpoint when he experienced marriage. He and his wife, Katherine von Bora, enjoyed a good marriage.

The negative view of sex perpetrated by the Jansenist and Puritan movements has had a profound influence on both Catholics and Protestants, but so has the idealism of the Romantics. Marriage and sexuality have, throughout history, been simultaneously devalued and idealized, but neither pessimism nor idealism proves solid foundations for the reality of marriage. It is little wonder that couples often come to marriage with conflicting ideas about the meaning of marriage and sexuality.

I do not suggest that couples run out and get a degree in theology before getting married. In fact, given the history of Christian theology, this probably wouldn't help! I do suggest that couples think about and talk about the meaning marriage has for them. Most Christians view marriage as an important spiritual union. In marriage, you minister to each other.

At the wedding, it is not the minister or priest who performs the ceremony, but the couple. Therefore you, the true ministers of this sacred event, need to prepare to enter into marriage. You will need to allow yourself some time for reflection. If you don't have time to reflect, you don't have time to be married. You are moving too fast. Slow down. This is a big step you're taking. As a therapist, I have been amazed at the number of people who fly into marriage, in the heat of intense emotion, with less thought than they would give to obtaining a pet or choosing a career. Pets and careers are more easily, and less injuriously, changed than spouses.

Don't be surprised if, upon reflection, you find yourself a bit confused and you occasionally struggle with conflicting ideas and emotions. You are in good company. Your understanding will be imperfect, but it will be a beginning and will develop over time. It is not within the scope of this book to discuss interfaith marriages in any depth, but I need to acknowledge that many couples will come together from different religious and cultural backgrounds. These differences can create conflict both during the wedding preparations and in marriage. Use this time to explore your common ground. Be sensitive to the other's needs and beliefs and honest about your own.

The image of marriage that has been the most helpful in my own marriage is central to both the Hebrew and Christian scriptures. The Hebrew scriptures describe God's covenant as a marriage (read Isaiah 54:5-6, 62:4-5) and the Christian scriptures use marriage as a symbol of Christ's relationship with the Church (read Ephesians 5:31-33). This image helps me on a practical level. When I want a guide for how I should relate to my husband, I ask myself: Does this particular action I am taking or this decision I am making reflect the kind of love God has for me? In other words, would God treat me the way I am treating my spouse? This has been a simple and effective guideline for me.

Our beliefs guide our choices. I believe that I am called to be as faithful to my spouse as Christ is faithful to the Church. I believe that the consummation of Christ's marriage to the Church (his death and resurrection) brought into human experience a third person, the Holy Spirit. I believe that our union, like the union of Christ with the Church, calls for deaths and risings, and our love, like the love between Christ and the Church, is essentially creative, not only in the co-creation of children but in the re-creation of ourselves. I believe that the Church needs my marriage, and that Christ needs my marriage, as an ongoing sign of God's love for his people. These key beliefs have profoundly affected the kind of marriage we have shared over the past twenty-five years.

What do you believe? Is there a particular image or scripture that speaks to you? Many wonderful books and scriptures offer guidance. Try reading and reflecting on the love chapter of 1 Corinthians (chapter 13), or on Ephesians 4 or 1 John 3. Ask married couples you know what thoughts, images and readings have inspired them. Then, when you have taken the time to think about what you believe, let your wedding reflect your beliefs.

It is no small feat to stay focused on your deepest and truest beliefs about marriage when preparing for your wedding. Weddings have become big business and high stress affairs, but you do *not* need to let the values of the merchants dictate or design your wedding. Nor do you need to let your fears of failure or your sense of inadequacy determine your wedding experience. Let your wedding issue not from your fears but from your faith. How? Nurture your faith in this time of preparation by taking daily time for reflection and prayer, worshipping together, spending quiet time together, and spending time with the people whose marriages you admire. Their positive attitudes will influence you. This is particularly important for people whose own parents have divorced.

Contemporary weddings often cost a small fortune, but a wedding does not need to be expensive to be meaningful and pleasurable, and price is no measure of love. The modern tendency to spend so much on weddings may at its core betray a contemporary superstition. Do we think that if we spend lots of money we are more likely to have a happy marriage? In agrarian societies, people threw grain at the couple to bring them luck. Do we subtly throw money at the ceremony in order to ensure marital bliss? Though weddings mean a great deal to my family, most of them have been remarkably inexpensive, all have been on the large side (because there are a lot of us) and all have been truly wonderful celebrations. As we go along, I will share suggestions on how to cut costs and stress without diminishing the joy of the occasion.

Where will you have your wedding? The first "marriage" took place in a garden, the garden of Eden. Many marriages still take place in gardens and some in homes, but most take place in houses of worship, in synagogues and churches. Where you choose to have your wedding says something about what you believe. If you believe that your marriage is a purely private affair and no one's business but your own, it doesn't make sense to have your wedding in a church.

Traditionally, Christian marriage celebrates not just two individuals, but the entire Church community. The power of the traditional church wedding is the power of the community. If your marriage is to survive the challenges of life, you will need other people along the way, people who share your values. A church wedding acknowledges this need and presents an opportunity to experience community support from the beginning. Each religious community has its liturgy. The leaders of your religious community are your best resource for liturgical traditions.

Sometimes couples try to turn a community event into a private event. This can lead to frustration, confusion and unnecessary stress. But the communal nature of a church wedding does not preclude making your wedding personal. A wedding can easily be both personal and communal, but it cannot easily be both communal and private.

For example, on one of our first dates I invited Matt to dinner (believing that the best way to a man's heart is through his stomach). He brought along a record in a medieval music record jacket and put it on before we sat down to eat. Instead of the medieval music that I expected, I was surprised to hear Elvis singing, "You ain't nothin' but a hound dog." Naturally, my future spouse enjoyed his joke and my surprise. Now this Elvis song has a personal meaning for us, but it would have no meaning for the community and would not be appropriate for the liturgy. My husband and I chose a favorite piece, Bach's "Gigue Fugue," instead of Elvis, for our recessional. A piece of music can have a personal meaning and simultaneously speak to the community. In your wedding liturgy, be aware that the liturgy is for the community, both those in attendance and the larger Christian community. This awareness will enhance your personal experience.

Countless wedding rituals, somber and silly, evoke every emotion from tears to laughter. There are clothing traditions, party traditions, traditions that involve breaking things and throwing things, fertility traditions, traditions to evoke good luck and protect from evil, traditions of giving and traditions of receiving, traditions of water and fire, and of course, traditions of food and drink.

Clothing Traditions

The modern American bride most often chooses a formal white dress, and the groom chooses a tux. White symbolizes purity. The bride wears "something blue" (an Israeli tradition) because blue symbolizes truth.[3] Armenian, Chinese and Turkish brides traditionally wore red, and Spanish brides dressed in black silk with lace mantillas. A Breton bride wore a silk sash with double loops that her mother would cut just before the wedding procession began. The mother would then embrace her daughter and make a little speech expressing her sorrow at parting from her daughter and blessing her. In Armenia, the wedding garments were blessed before the wedding.[4]

Two of my friends, a Chinese American and an Irish American, had two weddings: a church wedding for which the bride wore white, and an outdoor wedding for which the bride wore a red silk chipao with quantities of gold and jade jewelry. In this way they honored both his cultural background and hers. You may wish to choose traditions that reflect the diverse backgrounds your union brings together. As you make these decisions, seek a common ground that embraces the primary values you share. Respect your partner's desires and discomforts; be willing to compromise.

You can purchase your wedding garments, make them yourself, rent them or borrow them from friends or relatives. The borrowing of a gown can be meaningful as well as economical if the friend or relative has a marriage you admire. If you want a handmade gown and you are not handy with a needle and thread, have a relative or even a seamstress make one for you. Seamstresses are often surprisingly inexpensive. My mother-in-law made my gown out of white French batiste, embroidering the sleeves with Celtic symbols of marriage. A friend made lace for the tiers of the skirt. The dining room of my future in-laws was filled with patterns, fine batiste, lace and happy activity for weeks. I wanted to be able to dance freely at my wedding, so I chose a pattern with a full, ankle-length skirt, rather than a more formal gown with a train. Friends and family invested their talents and time, making the gown even more special for me.

I made a shirt for my husband, embroidering it with symbols of marriage. This custom has roots in Spain as well as in some parts of Scandinavia. The Spanish bride made the groom's shirt, showing off her needlework skills with embroidery and elaborate tucking. The Scandinavian groom wore the fine shirt his bride had made only twice: on the day of his wedding and on the day of his burial.

My mother-in-law created a wonderful tradition. She bought extra yardage of the batiste and put it away. When our first child was born, she used this batiste from my bridal dress to make a lovely baptismal gown. We used this baptismal gown for the baptism of both our children and have put it away for their children. If you, or a friend or family member, wish to make either a bridal gown or a groom's wedding shirt, excellent patterns are available in most fabric stores. I include here a few embroidery patterns traditional for weddings, which you might wish to use.

Figure 1: Scottish Crowned Heart
This is the Scottish symbol of marriage, which I used at my own wedding. Work in white on white in an outline stitch, such as a chain stitch or whipped running stitch. It works well as a decoration for long, full sleeves, or embroidered onto the ring pillow. If you use it for a ring pillow, tack a narrow satin ribbon where the two hearts join. Tie the rings onto the pillow with the ribbon.

Figure 2: Pennsylvania Dutch Love Birds
Outline birds and heart in chain or whipped running stitch. Use a satin stitch for wings, breast and heart. Use French Knots for the eyes and wing decoration. Make wings and eyes dark blue. Use a light rose or pink for the bird's breast. Use a deep rose or red for the heart and wing decorations (French knots). This design works well for a ring pillow. Attach a narrow satin ribbon to the center of the heart to tie the rings.

Figure 3: Chinese Cross Stitch Border
This is traditionally worked in blue cotton on white. The character for double happiness alternates with a stylized peony, symbol of love. The border design can be used at the hem of a dress or shirt or on the cuffs of either garment.

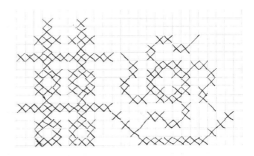

Another tradition, common to many ethnic groups, is the tradition of crowning. We even read about this ancient tradition in Song of Solomon 3:11, where King Solomon wears "the crown with which his mother crowned him on the day of his wedding, on the day of the gladness of his heart." The early Christian Church included crowning in the marriage rite, and it is still a part of the ceremony in Rome, Greece, Norway, Lithuania and Sweden. The bride and groom are crowned both in acknowledgment of the victory they have achieved in their union and of their new role as king and queen of their home.

In the Eastern Church, nuptial wreaths may be made of olive sprays and white and purple flowers, and placed on the heads of the bride and groom. Or crowns may be made of orange blossoms tied together with ribbons, symbolizing the couple's unity. Sometimes the crowns are made of decorated metal. In the Eastern Orthodox ritual, the crowning leads into the dance of Isaiah, joyfully danced by the bride, groom and sponsor (often the best man and/or maid of honor) three times encircling the little altar at the foot of the inner sanctuary. The Lithuanian tradition includes the passing on of the wreath, symbolic of the woman's transition from maiden to matron. The Norwegian bride is expected to "dance off her crown" after the wedding feast, a practice rather like throwing the bridal bouquet. The bride is blindfolded and surrounded by unattached young ladies who dance in a circle around her. The bride must, somehow or other, place her wreath on the head of one of these dancing women.

An interesting example of how a tradition can be reworked and adapted to fit current beliefs and values is an adaptation of the "capping" tradition still practiced by many Czech and Polish Americans. In the former Czechoslovakia and in Poland, a bride's transition from maiden to matron was marked by a ritual in which the bridesmaids removed the bride's wreath (often made of rosemary) and the bride's mother replaced it with a lace cap. This was a bittersweet occasion, often accompanied by the singing of melancholy songs, denoting the end of a carefree girlhood and the beginning of wifely responsibilities. As long hair has had sexual connotations from ancient times, the covering of the bride's long hair beneath the cap also symbolized the loss of virginity and her future role of mother.

Between 1880 and 1930, seventeen million immigrants came to the United States. Traditional clothing was often abandoned and current American styles adopted to help the immigrants "fit in." In Chicago, home to a large number of Slavic immigrants and to the largest Polish population outside of Warsaw, many traditions were preserved and adapted to fit the styles of the immigrants' new home. Czech and Polish brides of this period typically wore the white veil popular among American brides, but with a colored dress, which was both more practical (as the colored dress could be worn again) and simultaneously reminiscent of ethnic wedding clothing.

The traditional capping ceremony was eventually replaced by a kitchen apron ceremony. The symbolic function of the apron, which covered and "protected" the sexual organs, dates from Neolithic times. Like the cap, the apron carried a dual meaning, denoting both the woman's transition from virgin to sexual partner and mother and the taking on of wifely responsibilities. These aprons were often made by the godmother and decorated with symbols of marriage.

In the American tradition, the groom was sometimes included in the ritual and would hold a doll wrapped in a blanket. Some brides shook wooden spoons at the grooms, and the groom might be given such household objects as brooms and even drain plungers to suggest his future responsibilities.[5] In this way, the young couple recognize that marriage is more than romance. There are meals to be cooked, babies to be changed and drains to be unplugged. You can see how these rituals provided opportunity for humor. Some modern brides may dislike the emphasis on domesticity, and yet homemaking is an integral part of a marriage. Such traditions are easily adapted to fit a contemporary couple's view of equality and shared responsibility.

The bridal veil tradition has numerous roots and variations. At one time people thought the bridal veil protected the bride from evil. In the early Christian church, the veil sometimes substituted for the canopy, or *chuppah*, still used in Jewish wedding ceremonies. Many Swedish brides were married under a shawl. In Catholic ceremonies in many countries, a carecloth of fine linen is still placed over the couple's heads. Spanish brides wore beautiful black lace mantillas, and Mexican brides wore white veils with orange blossoms. In Scotland, a bridal handkerchief is held over the bride's head.

Although I did not have it held over my head, I did carry my great-grandmother's finely embroidered wedding handkerchief for my wedding (as did my sisters-in-law). I found it helped me, as I entered on such a wondrous and difficult enterprise as marriage, to hold on to something that reminded me of the many generations of couples before me who had successfully negotiated the same deep waters. Perhaps this psychological need is the origin of the tradition of carrying something old.

I knew a young woman who could not look to her own family for a tradition of happy marriages. She borrowed the wedding veil of a friend, who had had a long and successful marriage. For her, this friend's veil helped protect her from doubt and insecurity, much as our ancestors used the veil to protect them from evil spirits. Just as it is important to have traditions such as the Czech and Polish capping and aproning rituals to remind us of the earthly realities of marriage, so we need also to find traditions that help us experience the divine hope of Christian marriage. For this woman, her friend's veil reminded her of the joys of a successful marriage and thus helped her nurture her own very necessary sense of hope.

Jewelry often has significance in wedding traditions. The Chinese bride is likely to be resplendent with gold and jade, and the Spanish bride with gold, pearls and emeralds (given by the groom). The most prominent piece of jewelry, of course, is the wedding ring. Rings symbolize the couple's love and commitment to each other and have special importance because they will be worn, not for a day, but for a lifetime. The French often have their wedding rings made in two pieces with the groom's name on one piece, the bride's on the other and the date of their wedding on the joining piece.

Even the shoes the bridal couple wear can have significance. A Swedish bride wears slip-on shoes without buttons, strings, hooks or other fasteners, so that she will have an easy childbirth. Her father puts a piece of silver in her left shoe and her mother puts a piece of gold in her right as a symbol of their hopes for her prosperity.

Breaking and Throwing Traditions

I confess that I am partial to breaking and throwing traditions because they are a lot of fun and we are so seldom allowed to do it! How can breaking and throwing things be spiritual? First of all, two of the surest signs of the presence of God are inner peace and joy. If God is part of our relationship, then our celebration must be joyful.

Theologian Paul Tillich, reflecting on the gospel passage in which Mary pours oil on the feet of Jesus, suggests that as Christians we are called to live with abundant hearts, that our love should never be merely rational, but must overflow in "holy waste."[6] This abundance of heart that Tillich describes involves an irrational (or perhaps trans-rational) exuberance. These traditions insist that our joy and our love are so great that they cannot be contained, and we really must throw things and break things to express our feelings adequately. Because these breaking and throwing traditions involve doing something so out of the ordinary, they highlight the extraordinary quality of the event. We do not normally break things, but on our wedding day we do. Why? Because this is a special day.

Some of the breaking traditions symbolize the destruction of our old life of single-hood as we take on the new life of marriage. Other breaking traditions remind us of the fragility of human life. We must be joyful, yes, but if, even in our joy, we can remember our mortality and our human fragility, perhaps we can begin to understand that love is strong enough to bear the weight of both our joys and our sorrows. Perhaps we can begin to realize that love is eternal.

The tradition of throwing rice to wish the couple a fertile union comes to us from the Orient. The ancient Hebrews threw barley, and many other cultures throw grain or nuts. An updated version of the tradition of throwing grain is to crumble a piece of wedding cake over the bride's head. Bouquets, garters and flowers may also be thrown. A Moroccan groom throws an egg at his new wife, symbolizing his hopes that she will have an easy childbirth. (I have been unable to ascertain whether or not this is a raw egg. We hope it is a cooked one.)[7]

One custom involves throwing an old shoe, which may be the origin of the tradition of tying shoes to the bumper of the couple's car. Historically, the removal of a shoe confirmed a sale, so the custom may date back to the days when one purchased a bride. Traditionally, removing one's shoes indicated reverence. A person removed his or her sandals at Roman and Grecian shrines, and Moses removed his sandals when he was in God's presence.

In some parts of Germany, wedding parties throw every piece of already cracked or broken china and glass out the window. Many breaking traditions symbolize the consummation of the marriage and the bride's loss of virginity. One Slavic tradition involves breaking glasses against the door of the newly married couple's home while they were consummating their marriage. (I'm glad my four brothers hadn't heard of this tradition.) In India, a coconut is passed over the couple's heads three times and then broken on the ground. A Scottish tradition requires that one toast the couple, preferably with good whiskey, and toss the glasses into the fireplace. (My brothers had heard of this tradition but my mother strictly forbade practicing it.) The Jewish practice of breaking a wine glass is an ancient tradition. After the second sip of wine, the glass that the bride and groom have drunk from is wrapped in a towel and crushed by the groom, reminding all present of mortality.

Traditions of Fire and Water

It is virtually impossible to find an event of spiritual importance that does not include traditions concerning fire and water. These elements are so basic, necessary and central to human life that they continue to have great symbolic importance for us.

Water signifies cleansing and purity. Muslim, Jewish and Orthodox women ritually bathe before their weddings. Greek couples wash their hands and feet. Catholic couples may bless themselves with holy water before their marriage to remind them of their baptism and new life in Christ.

Fire brings light into darkness. Christ is the light of the world, and the Christian marriage can bring light not only into the lives of the couple but into the world. In ancient Rome, torches lit the bridal procession to and from the wedding. Many couples choose to have candlelight at their weddings or on the tables at their reception. A couple, after a joyful but fatiguing wedding celebration, might light a special candle purchased for the occasion (beeswax symbolizes purity and sweetness), pray together and bless each other before going to bed. Such a simple, light-filled moment can help one make the transition from the communal celebration to the private sharing of your love. Keep the candle and light it on each anniversary, blessing each other again, renewing your vows and thanking God for another year of marriage.

Prayer of Blessing

Grant that our wills may be so knit together in your will, and our spirits in your Spirit, that we may grow in love and peace with you and one another all the days of our life. Amen.

(The Book of Common Prayer)

Edible Traditions

Food is such a necessary and enjoyable part of life that a day without food is universally considered a day of penance. A wedding is a time of joy and therefore a time of feasting. There is a large number of foods associated with weddings, and a variety of occasions for eating them. Some feasts last a few hours, others a number of days.

In Germany the Polterabend, or rehearsal dinner, is an important occasion. The dinner is followed by entertainment, which might consist of a short play, operetta or charade, portraying the future life of the couple. The evening concludes with a dance. I have a Chinese friend whose rehearsal dinner consisted of a twelve-course banquet of traditional dishes (including a magnificent fish that stared at me throughout the feast).

Eating and drinking together is one of the oldest signs of union. In fact, it was the sign Jesus used at the Last Supper to reassure his followers that his love for them was eternal. The Greeks and Romans ate quince and pomegranate on the day of their weddings. In Germany, couples traditionally eat a bowl of soup together. A Greek couple eats a maize pudding together from the same plate. The Jewish couple shares a glass of wine. The French drink wine from a special two-handled cup. In Brittany, the couple shares white bread and brandy. In Japan, they share saki. In Brazil, they share a glass of brandy. The Chinese drink tea together, and the English drink ale. In fact, the word *bridal* may come from "bride-ale," referring to the wedding feast.[8] In Italy, the wedding couple sends sugared almonds to friends or guests. Many contemporary couples give out sugared almonds decoratively wrapped in netting and ribbon to guests at the reception. Couples often feed each other a piece of wedding cake. Perhaps the strangest food custom I came across was a custom from France. Some members of the wedding party visit the newly-weds in bed in the early morning hours, presenting them with a dish made of white wine, eggs, chocolate and biscuits, served in a chamber pot!

Good food and drink make your wedding a memorable and uplifting celebration. Does this mean that you have to hire expensive caterers in order to have a wonderful wedding? Of course not. My mother cooked all the food for our reception (to which 400 guests were invited), including two wedding cakes (a bride's cake and a groom's cake). She started cooking weeks ahead and put things away in the freezer. Her primary fear was that we would have a power failure and everything would defrost prematurely. Or, conversely, she feared that she would forget to take things out to defrost in time. Neither disaster occurred, fortunately. We had a delicious feast spread out on long tables, covered with burgundy cloth, in the shade of the oak trees on our front lawn.

Of course, as you may have gathered by now, my mother is an exceptional woman and a great cook, but even if you aren't a great cook, most of us know a great cook or two and, with the help of friends and family, a wonderful reception can be created. My brother and sister-in-law were on a shoestring budget for their wedding and welcomed the involvement of family and friends. A number of us chipped in to help prepare their wedding feast (it truly was a feast) and we had great fun doing so.

Each culture and community has its own traditional dishes, and some are shared by many countries. Finnish weddings include wedding rings, *avioliitopikkuleipa*, which are buttery cookie rings made like little sandwiches with strawberry jam. Dundee cake is traditional in Scotland, and Armenian weddings include a wedding pilaf with raisins and nuts. In France, the reception table is likely to boast a

Gougere, a beautiful pastry ring made with Gruyere cheese. Roast suckling pig is served at feasts throughout the world.

In my family, matrimonial bars are traditional. The origin of their name is lost in the mists of history, but fortunately the recipe is not. In preparation for our wedding, my mother was determined to fill a 25-pound tin with matrimonial bars. Every day she would make several batches and store them in the tin, carefully layered with waxed paper. But no matter how many she baked, she couldn't fill the tin. No one would admit to eating them. She put a dire warning, complete with skull and cross bones, on top of the tin, but still the cookies disappeared. In desperation, she hid the tin in the freezer. This led to the discovery that matrimonial bars are delicious frozen! She never did fill that 25-pound tin, but we managed to have plenty on hand for our wedding anyway. Matrimonial bars are easily made, keep well and are, perhaps, too popular with family and friends.

Matrimonial Bars

Mix together until crumbly:
- 2 cups flour
- 1 $\frac{1}{2}$ cup oatmeal
- 1 teaspoon baking soda
- 1 $\frac{1}{2}$ cup brown sugar
- $\frac{3}{4}$ cup butter

Spread half of the crumb mixture on the bottom of a baking pan. Cover with 1 jar of fruit jam (we prefer apricot or raspberry). Then spread the rest of the crumb mixture on top of the jam and pat down gently. Bake at 375 degrees for approximately 20 minutes. Cool and cut into bars.

Planning the food for your reception gives you a wonderful opportunity to share your joy in a personal and special way. The couple may want to make a special dish themselves to share with their friends. When my brother, a carpenter, married my husband's sister, the two of them built a gingerbread house together. It was a beautiful little cottage, complete with candy decorations and a family of little marzipan mice. It became the centerpiece for their reception table.

The wedding cake tradition goes back to pagan times, when a bride was fed a piece of sacred cake upon entering her new home as a way of introducing her to her new gods. Not only did a bride take her husband's name, she was expected to take on his religion.[9] Grain cakes served as sacrificial offerings to appease the gods.

The tradition of placing small figurines on the top of the cake hearkens back to the use of totems, small figures used to attract good spirits (or frighten away evil ones).

An English tradition of the 17th and 18th centuries of sending small pieces of wedding cake home with guests for "good luck" is still practiced. Young women would sleep with the cake under their pillows in the hopes of dreaming of their future spouse. For the Irish, fruit cake is a favorite. A honey cake is traditional in Greece. A child hides coins and a ring in the cake, so the guests must eat carefully! The one who finds the ring gives it to the groom in exchange for another ring or a small gift. Cakes are sometimes decorated with marzipan figures, flowers and fruit. In Italy, almond paste (marzipan) is called matrimony, as it joins the bitter with the sweet. Wedding cakes can also be decorated with flowers. My mother used marzipan flowers on the groom's cake and candied violets on the bride's cake. Chocolate flowers (easily made from molds) and frosting flowers are often used.

In America, wedding celebrations often include champagne. Whiskey, sake, tea, spiced mead and ale have all been popular drinks at weddings. Given concerns over drinking and driving and the number of recovering alcoholics among us, remember to provide nonalcoholic drinks as well. These can be just as festive as the alcoholic drinks. For a summer wedding, you might serve Rose Punch. For a winter wedding, Spiced Honey Grog is good. For the children, try serving pink lemonade with slices of lemon and fresh fruit.

Rose Punch

Mix together:
- 4 10-ounce packages of frozen raspberries, thawed
- 1 bottle of nonalcoholic rose wine
- 1 cup sugar

Let the punch stand at room temperature for an hour and then strain into a clear punch bowl. Add 4 6-ounce cans of frozen pink lemonade concentrate, stirring until thawed. Add 3 bottles of nonalcoholic champagne, 2 bottles of nonalcoholic rose wine, and sparkling water (optional). Add ice. Makes approximately 60 servings.

Spiced Honey Grog

Combine:

1 gallon of apple cider

1 cup of honey

juice of 4 oranges (reserving

4 thin slices of orange

to float on top)

1/2 cup butter

5 sticks of cinnamon

4 teaspoons grated

orange peel

1 teaspoon ground nutmeg

Bring to a boil and simmer 5 minutes, stirring occasionally. Makes approximately 50 servings.

Music and Dancing

From earliest times, wedding rituals included music and dance, which express and communicate our most powerful emotions. Some traditions involve dance in the wedding ceremony, such as the Greek dance of Isaiah, and virtually all traditions involve dancing at the wedding feast. You do not need to be a great dancer to have fun dancing at your wedding. Dancing, for most of us, is an expression of joy.

I remember a beautiful Hasidic wedding I attended on top of a hill in Berkeley, California. After the bride and groom were joined in matrimony beneath the white canopy, the canopy was dropped over them. The rabbi told us that while they were under that canopy their souls were joined in heaven, where they prayed for us and for all the world. He then invited us to pray for the couple by dancing. When we dance, he told us, we pray twice. We began to dance, forming long lines encircling the couple. The friend I was with had only one leg, and I remember how he danced beside me, held aloft in the rhythmic joy of that long line of dancers. The ceremony became the feast in a seamless act of dancing prayer.

I recall my brother and sister-in-law, elegantly attired, bopping to 50s rock and roll at their reception and the Scottish waltz my husband and I danced at ours. We do not often think of dancing as prayer, but when it celebrates our love and expresses our joy it speaks a divine language.

Sometimes dancing is also an amusing opportunity to engage in the compromise and struggle inevitable in marriage. I had been a dancer and could not imagine a wedding party without dancing. Unfortunately, my husband hates to dance (no one's perfect). Out of deference for my desires, he agreed to dance a waltz with me. In appreciation of his discomfort I didn't nag him into dancing more than that one dance. We had great fun (at least I did) in the weeks preceding our wedding as I taught him the steps to this dance. One couple I know took dance lessons prior to their wedding. The weeks of learning to coordinate dance steps together became, for my friend, symbolic of the process their relationship went through as they practiced moving together, occasionally stepping on each other's toes, at times arguing over who was leading whom.

Again, bringing in ethnic traditions can add to the fun. Usually the traditions will reflect the roots of the couple, but sometimes the guests may add their personal gifts to the celebration. We had Scottish dancing and Irish music at our wedding, representative of our backgrounds; but one of the most memorable moments at our reception was a dance, performed by a close friend, from a tradition foreign to both my husband and me. This friend is Chinese American, and she danced a traditional ribbon dance as a gift to us. It was nearing dusk, not long before we were to depart on our honeymoon. A contented quiet had descended on the gathering as we all lazed about trying to digest the quantities of food we had eaten. Anna, with her long dark hair in two braids down her back and sticks with long ribbons in either hand, began to dance. As Anna danced, the ribbons encircled the air in graceful swirls of color. It was a magical moment. Involve your friends and family in the celebration. Think about the people in your life. What special gifts do they have to offer?

Being married to a musician (and being an amateur musician myself), I have a great appreciation for the importance of music in the wedding celebration. Both the reception and the wedding liturgy are times when good music can communicate a depth of beauty and joy that mere words cannot convey. In the United States, when we think of wedding music, we are likely to think of Mendelssohn's music, originally composed to accompany Shakespeare's *Midsummer Night's Dream*, and of Wagner's piece from *Lohengrin*. The Mendelssohn piece accompanies a scene in which Bottom is transformed into a jackass, and Wagner's music precedes a scene in which the bridegroom murders his rival and abandons his bride. These associations don't bother many people, but I personally favor other pieces. Your faith community can help you choose music that expresses the spiritual and communal nature of your wedding celebration. Let the music for your reception express your joy.

Herb and Flower Traditions

Plants and flowers add to wedding festivities, both as decoration and as symbols of life, purity and beauty. Bouquets of flowers cover church and reception tables, bridal crowns are often made of flowers or herbs, and bridal veils may be ornamented with flowers. In the early Christian Church, bride and groom were crowned with myrtle. Chinese, Mexican and Spanish brides wear orange blossoms and Slavic brides often wear rosemary. Roses mixed with delicate white baby's breath symbolize love for many American brides. One tradition invites the bride to remove the groom's boutonniere and place it in her hair before the first dance at the wedding reception. The tradition of flower girls strewing petals before the bridal procession is an updated version of an ancient tradition in which children carried bunches of grain to symbolize fertility.

A lovely tradition still popular in many Catholic ceremonies honors Mary, the mother of Jesus. The bride, looking to Mary as the model for a Christian wife, places her bouquet before a statue of Mary toward the end of the liturgy. Before placing the bouquet at Mary's feet, the bride may kneel and offer a brief silent prayer, requesting Mary's blessing and guidance. Usually the maid of honor carries a second bouquet for the bouquet-tossing at the reception. In the Greek Church, bride and groom prostrate themselves before a picture of Mary and the congregation sings the hymn "Let Israel Rejoice."

In Bermuda, many couples plant a tree at the time of marriage. This wonderful ritual, with the ensuing care and the ongoing growth, serve as an eloquent reminder of the care and faithfulness a marriage requires. If you wish to plant a tree to celebrate your union, pick a hardy one and ask your local nursery about its soil and light requirements. A dying tree could be a disheartening symbol. A bonsai tree might make a good substitute for apartment dwellers, but if you want to try to grow a bonsai, expect a few plants to die in the process. Recognize that the symbolism involves the process of learning to grow something, not just having a thriving tree.

Remembering the Poor and Deceased

We have already mentioned a number of traditions that remind us in the midst of our joy of the realities of life's struggles and sorrows. Though weddings have historically included this element, contemporary American weddings rarely include it. The elimination of this tradition says something about our culture that, in the pursuit of happiness, purposefully puts everything unpleasant out of sight and out of mind. Disagreeable experiences are expunged from our memories; undesirable people are not allowed to live in our neighborhoods. And what is the result? The result is that when a couple runs into some unpleasantness (and the nicest and luckiest of couples inevitably will), they are inclined to think something is wrong with their relationship.

I remember when my husband and I encountered such a valley in our relationship (it felt more like a pit at the time). One friend advised me to get a divorce. While divorce is sometimes inevitable and even advisable, far too often it serves as a quick cure for unhappiness, when a less destructive cure is available. We tend to view difficulties as threats to marriage when, in fact, they often stimulate the growth of intimacy and result, not in separation and estrangement, but in deeper love and greater understanding. It is, therefore, not inappropriate to remind a couple entering into marriage that sorrow, death and poverty exist, and that acknowledging their existence does not diminish or threaten our love.

In a Breton tradition of remembrance, an old woman walks up to the new couple at the wedding reception, kneels before them and chants the De Profundis, the prayer of the dead. This is a Christian version of the invocation to the spirits of dead ancestors, invited to bless the new marriage. Korean, Japanese and Chinese couples pray at the tombs of deceased relatives. At our reception, a piper played "The Flowers of the Forest," a melancholy Scottish tune traditionally played in memory of those loved ones who have died during the year.

Such traditions can be especially powerful when a significant family member has died. Acknowledging their absence and giving people a moment to remember, mourn and honor them, can enhance rather than lessen the joy of the celebration. Part of the great mystery of love is its ability to contain sorrow without being diminished.

Such traditions also serve to root us by linking us to the past. A contemporary couple can do this by displaying family photos at the reception. My brother and my husband's sister married not long after her mother's death. Although it was a bright joyful day, it was inevitable that all of us, and especially Maria, would miss Joan's presence. On a large bulletin board at the reception we displayed photos from both sides of the family: childhood photos of the couple, their parents, grandparents and even great-grandparents. These photos inspired delightful reminiscing, and the ache of loss was somehow assuaged by the reciting of poignant, funny and happy memories.

Another tradition we would do well to revive calls for giving alms to the poor. In France, the bridesmaids, *les demoiselles d'honneur*, collected alms for the poor. In Germany, the bride distributed alms to the poor. In Sweden, portions of each dish served at the wedding feast were saved and given to the needy. We live in a consumer society that constantly bombards us with advertisements enticing us to buy and encouraging us to measure our worth by what we have bought. It is not always easy, given our freedom and our materialism, to choose to be people who live for others, yet as Christians this is what we are called to be.

In the past, alms were often given to the poor to ensure the prosperity of the couple. Today, we might give to the poor to assert and secure our own Christian values and our spiritual sanity in a world too often at odds with these values. A couple, before their wedding, might want to spend some time together volunteering with a service organization. In a concrete and visible way, this couple declares that their love calls them to be present to the needs of each other and to the needs of their world.

Odds and Ends

The bridal shower, where friends shower the bride with gifts, is a party tradition popular in the United States. Its origin is attributed to a stubborn Dutch father who refused to give his daughter a dowry. It seems she wanted to marry a miller whose habit of giving bread and flour to the poor left him short of funds. The father had his heart set on his daughter marrying a pig farmer who owned 100 pigs. The daughter was, apparently, every bit as stubborn as her father, and wouldn't give the wealthy pig farmer the time of day. When the people who had been aided by the generous miller found out about the couple's plight, they got together and decided each to give a simple but practical present. Of course, the subsequent showering of presents from the miller's grateful friends proved more generous than the dowry the father would have given. I suspect the father was a bit stingy. The story suggests that one's own generosity is a good foundation for marriage and that the support of one's friends is more vital than the price tag on the present.

In the Song of Solomon (2:4) we read, "He brought me to his banquet hall and raised the banner of love over me" (Today's English Version). This may refer to the canopy or to a banner. Banners and flags are an old tradition and provide a festive touch at the wedding reception. My mother made banners that my father somehow managed to hang from the tall stately oaks in our front yard. I remember the banners floating above us as we ate and ate and ate. For Phil and Maria's reception at our house in San Francisco, we hung the wedding banners out of the upper-story windows. (This had an extra benefit as, in order to hang the banners, Uncle Jack had to unstick the windows, which hadn't opened in years!) In our current home in Oak Park, Illinois, it is customary to fly house flags for special events, including weddings. Flags can be purchased or made from sturdy material. Bright colors and simple symbolic designs (intertwined rings, flowers, the claddagh, hearts, doves, etc.) work well.

Blessings are also traditional. The priest or minister blesses the couple. Sometimes the couple's new home or bedroom is blessed. In many cultures, parents bless their children. The bride and groom may bless each other. These blessings may be simple or elaborate, taken from scripture or Christian tradition, or created for the occasion. The one giving the blessing places his or her hands on the head of the person being blessed. Or the blessing can be given with the sign of the cross traced on the person's forehead.

The tradition of jumping over a broomstick was common in the South, especially as a ritual in slave marriages. Oddly enough, the tradition also appears among British railroad construction workers and in Wales. Often the ritual became part of a Christian wedding ceremony. In some rituals, the couple held hands and jumped together over the broom three times; in others, the bride and groom each had a broom they stepped over. Sometimes the broom was laid across the sill of the house for the couple to step over before entering their home together.

The exact meaning of the ritual is unclear, although it appears it was thought to seal the marriage and bring good luck. Josephine Anderson, who grew up as a slave in Florida, gives an interesting explanation. She claims that it is well known that witches have to count everything, so when you put the broom on the floor, the witch has to stop and count every straw. The witch will be so busy counting straws she won't bother the new couple.[10]

Is this a superstition? Of course. But let's not dismiss it too readily. Reflect for a moment on what it must have been like for slaves to marry. Their owners had the power to separate them, to take away their children and to enjoy the sexual favors of the wife, and the couple was powerless to intervene. The witch symbolizes evil, and these couples were clearly dealing with evil. In the story of the witch, the evil that threatens the couple is made to look absurd, petty and ultimately powerless.

In this tradition, the couple is being told that evil is really only an obsessive, compulsive old witch, easily distracted by a common broom. Is this so far from our beliefs? We believe that there is evil in the world and that we will sometimes be powerless in the face of that evil. We believe that evil cannot conquer God, who is the source of all goodness. When faced with evil, we need to be reassured that it is not more powerful than good, although it may appear so at times.

What if a young couple wanted to step over a broom in memory of their ancestors and in gratitude for the strength and faith that enabled so many slave marriages to endure so much? Would this be superstition? If the couple believes that they can control the forces of evil by jumping over a broom, yes. But if they understand that it wasn't magic that enabled so many of these slaves to live lives of love against immense odds, if the broom symbolizes for them the survival of love in an atmosphere of hate, then we are no longer talking about superstition. The power that tradition has in our lives ultimately resides not in what it has meant to others in the past, but in what we allow it to mean for us today. Our past is part of us and we dare not ignore it, but ultimately we must make it our own. In so doing we may alter the tradition. Certainly, the tradition will alter us.

The Honeymoon

The word *honeymoon* comes from the French, *lune de miel*, literally, moon of honey, and refers to a French custom in which the couple drank a special honey wine for a month after the wedding. Today, the honeymoon provides space for couples to spend uninterrupted time together, adjusting to their new life, enjoying each other's presence, and recovering from the fatiguing wedding preparations and celebrations.

Your honeymoon is a good time to acknowledge the profound changes that marriage brings and to reflect on the meaning your marriage has for you. Consider looking together, on a hike or in shops, for some item that will symbolize your marriage. You need to agree on the symbol, and it needs to be something you can keep in your home. A patchwork quilt might symbolize your desire to create unity from the parts of yourselves; a picture of a rainbow might speak of your hopefulness; an empty bowl could remind you of your commitment to be open; a crucifix might express your willingness to sacrifice for one another.

In marriage we minister to each other in intimate ways. During your honeymoon, explore different ways to tend to one another's physical, emotional and spiritual needs. Try creating a prayer tradition to use on future anniversaries. Read one of the scriptures from your wedding together, alternating reading verses. Then sit facing each other with eyes closed. In this shared stillness, ask nothing for yourself but pray only for your partner: prayers of petition, prayers of thanksgiving, prayers from the heart.

From a spiritual perspective, times of transition are marked by traditions that allow us to set aside time to reflect, to pray and to adjust to the changes the transition requires us to make. Even if you have spent a great deal of time in dialogue, you are likely to find that the commitment you have just made will alter your relationship, sometimes subtly, sometimes dramatically. The honeymoon gives us a little time to focus on our relationship.

Keeping Love Alive

How does a couple survive disappointment, change, boredom, conflict and the daily irritations of shared life? I believe divine grace has a lot to do with it, along with hard work, lots of support and a sense of humor. What traditions can help us keep our love alive? A tradition, as defined by Webster's, is "an inherited, established, or customary thought or action." Traditions that keep love alive are those customary thoughts and actions that promote good communication, encourage us to celebrate our love and help us to stay focused on Christian values. In fact, the very traditions that helped us to develop our love will keep our love alive: an evening stroll, leisurely conversations over coffee, rides in the wine country, picnics, sharing our thoughts on various books. Problems arise because, while courtship motivates us to take time for each other, the post-wedding distractions of daily life and the constancy of togetherness frequently make time together seem less of a priority. In fact, we become complacent.

Inward Priorities

As Americans, often our most precious commodity is time. We can measure how important something is to us by the amount of time we invest in it. For many of us, particularly those living two-job marriages, we will need to schedule time to be together or it won't happen. Our employers, quite naturally, arrange our work schedules for their convenience, not for the well-being of our families. You will need to assert the priority of your relationship.

On numerous occasions I have told employers from the beginning that I couldn't work on Fridays as it is my husband's only day off, only to find myself scheduled for Fridays. My husband works for the Church, which one expects to value family life; but his employers in the Christian community have sometimes been less supportive of family life than my employers in the secular world. It is difficult to assert ourselves with employers. We want to be flexible and keep our jobs, so we are likely to give our marriages the short end of the stick. Sometimes economic necessity dictates our choices, but often it is simply easier to make career the priority. Spouses are often more accommodating than employers.

There have been periods in our marriage when my husband and I didn't have a day off together. I was off work on weekends and holidays, while my husband, a church musician, worked six days a week, weekends and most holidays. During these times we made a practice of meeting for lunch or having a leisurely breakfast together on the days he went in late. We didn't have as much time as we would have liked, but we regularly spent some time together and we made the most of the time we had.

Outward Expressions

It is important, for the survival of your own love, that your love be shared. Most of us will share our love in a profound way through the bearing and rearing of children; but all marriages, those with and those without children, will be stronger for being generous. Create traditions of giving. There are many ways to be there for others. Follow a simple Jewish tradition: Keep a box in your home in which to collect money for those in need. Jews call this box a *tzedakah*, or charity box, because it faithfully reminds us of our obligations to society. Many Jews put money into the tzedakah box before praying. Sign up for a charity walkathon. Become a tutor with a literacy program or a volunteer with an organization such as Habitat for Humanity. Teach at your church; visit newcomers to your neighborhood; read for the elderly at a nursing home. Do it together and do it for others. Love given helps love grow.

A couple needs time together, and we need time to be apart. We need to nurture both our personal spirituality and our shared spirituality. My family can easily tell if I have neglected my personal prayer life. I become more irritable, more stressed out and a lot harder to be around. I need to have a regular time set aside for personal prayer. Be aware of your personal spiritual needs and make sure they get met.

To nurture your shared spirituality, pray together. Earlier I mentioned the couple who begin each morning with a brief moment of silence while they hold hands. Sure, you might be embarrassed the first few times you try it, but what a simple way to communicate your mutual affection. Have a certain night on which you read scripture together and discuss how it relates to you. Or set aside a special time to say the rosary together or Morning or Evening Prayer. Join a Bible study together. Get active in your faith community. Participate in the sacraments. Say grace together before your meals (and arrange to eat at least one meal together each day). Make a retreat as a couple. Most retreat houses offer retreats for couples. You wouldn't expect your garden to survive without water; don't expect your marriage to survive without a constant infusion of grace.

Have fun together. Take one afternoon a week to do something silly. Play miniature golf, fly a kite, go roller-skating, take dance lessons. Different seasons of your relationship call for different traditions. At one point in our marriage, my husband and I had a standing date for lunch. I would pick the place (it had to be cheap, a place we'd never been to before, and a place with personality). These get-togethers were not times to discuss money matters or pet peeves. They were a time to joke, to dream and to simply enjoy each other's company. We need time to talk about serious issues, but we also need time to be frivolous together.

Community Support

Closed marriages, that is, marriages that are walled in and sealed off from the community, quickly become unhealthy marriages. Create traditions that will help you have a marriage open to the support of others. Have one night a month when you invite other couples over for dinner; it can be a fancy sit-down dinner, pizza or a barbecue. The neighbors on our block periodically get together for a progressive dinner, going from house to house for different courses. Our last progressive dinner had an Italian theme with food and music to match. We chatted and discussed our gardens and the local schools while listening to Italian opera and Frank Sinatra.

When we lived in Detroit, I used to call up our neighbors at the last minute and invite them over for impromptu potlucks. Each couple brought a dish they were intending for their own meal. We frequently had up to forty people at these informal affairs. There were certain rules. You were not allowed to dress up, and the host was forbidden to clean house or discuss housekeeping. As our neighborhood was in a run-down historic district in the inner city, we were all much involved in rehabilitating our lovely old decrepit houses, so it was permissible to discuss plumbing repair, plastering, refinishing and the like.

Getting together regularly with members of your own sex can be a good way to get outside support. In Detroit, the women of the neighborhood had a "sewing circle." We were a diverse group of full-time homemakers, a lawyer, a psychologist, two teachers and a sociologist. The discussions were lively and sometimes we even sewed. We drank tea, ate cookies, worked on our various projects, and chatted about our lives, our dreams, our children, and, of course, our men. Our sewing circle helped us connect with other women dealing with the same daily issues. Getting support outside of the home enabled us to be more supportive within the home.

Private Space

We are influenced by our surroundings. Let your home reflect both your personalities and your beliefs. Let it radiate the spirit of love that brought you together. You might hang a cross or crucifix on the wall, place a family Bible on a table, a statue of Mary in the kitchen (a Slavic tradition), a picture of a favorite saint in your bedroom, or frame a meaningful quotation and set it on the mantel. Fill your house with pictures of the people you love. Surround yourself with objects that remind you of your deepest held values. Let them constantly tell you who you are and what you believe. Our society is not always supportive of our religious beliefs, so sometimes we may wish to hide our faith in order to fit in, to make our homes reflect the values of others, rather than our own values. Let your values be visible. It will make it easier to live by them.

Sexual Expression

Sexual relations can be one of the most enjoyable and most difficult parts of a relationship, but the popular notion that sexual enjoyment declines with age and familiarity is an idea that many married couples (myself included) would challenge. Sexual enjoyment can increase with experience and greater emotional intimacy. The hormonal infatuation of youth pales in comparison with the mature sharing of one's sexuality with a lover you have known for many years.

As a therapist, I find that most of the people who come to me with marital problems are suffering from poor communication, addictions and/or infidelity. Substance abuse and infidelity are serious problems that require outside help. A good therapist, twelve-step programs and support groups can be invaluable helps to couples dealing with these issues. Most of the less serious marital difficulties I encounter stem from poor communication, particularly true in regard to sexual issues.

Many of us have trouble learning how to talk about sex, even with our lovers. Much of our sexual communication (and miscommunication) is on a nonverbal level and has been reduced to mere habits. That is, I look at you in a certain way, or you come up and put your arms around me while I'm washing the dishes, or I put on a lacy negligee, or you rub the back of my neck, and we expect the other to know that we want to have sex. If there is no response, or if there is the "wrong response," we are likely to feel inadequate, insecure, angry or hurt.

What has this got to do with spiritual traditions? Sex is a deeply spiritual act, nurturing not only the body but the soul. Our habitual nonverbal cues, good or bad, are traditions. If I always put on the lavender negligee, light scented candles, play a certain CD or turn off the lights when I want sex, these customary actions or signals become intimate traditions. Virtually all married couples have these little traditions. If you don't have intimate traditions, or the ones you have are unhealthy or unsatisfying to either partner, create good ones.

We can express our desires with a touch, with flowers, candles, music, clothing, even with food. Cooking your spouse's favorite meal and serving it by candlelight sends a message. Couples need to have personal ways of saying not only when they want sex, but how they want sex. Saying it with words communicates the desire, but saying it with candlelight and soft music also sets the mood not only by creating a conducive atmosphere, but also by recalling to memory other experiences of intimacy. We have trouble sexually when we ignore or misunderstand these intimate traditions. Pay attention to the way your lover customarily communicates his or her sexual needs and desires. If your lover doesn't understand your non-verbal communication, don't fall into the "if you loved me you'd understand" trap. If you love your partner, you won't require him or her to be a mind reader. It's lovely to be able to communicate without words but it's naive and a little immature to expect to do so all the time.

For most couples, simple fatigue and distractions can spoil a good sex life. Don't expect to have great sex when you're worn out or have a million things on your mind. If you are always worn out and distracted, make some changes in how you live. Build in some intimate traditions (a massage, a hot bath, soft music) that will help you relax and get in the mood.

Celebrating Love

Celebrate your relationship by making a big deal out of your anniversaries (and for heaven's sake don't forget them). Arrange to get off work early and have an intimate afternoon together. Go to a special restaurant. Go out dancing. Spend the night somewhere romantic. Revisit the place where you spent your honeymoon. Write your spouse a thank-you note. Let your anniversary be a time of gratitude. Some couples like to mark special anniversaries (perhaps your tenth, your twenty-fifth, your fiftieth) by taking second honeymoons or renewing their vows. If you want to renew your vows, check with your church community or create your own celebration at home.

Learn from the hard times. Rejoice in the good times. And above all, believe in your marriage; both in your ability to grow together in love and in God's ability to guide you.

4

In the Beginning:
Birthing and Blessings

One of my worst moments as a therapist occurred twenty years ago when I was just getting started. I was working as a family therapist for an inpatient treatment program for chemical dependency. An attractive young woman and her two lovely daughters, aged 6 and 8, had come to me for counseling while her husband was in treatment. Not surprisingly, the children had been neglected emotionally as their parents struggled with the devastating effects of addiction. The entire family was oriented to placating, avoiding and attending to the needs of the addict while the needs of other family members went unnoticed and unmet. In an attempt to re-focus the family and to begin strengthening the relationship between the mother and her daughters, I suggested that the mother affirm each of her daughters by naming something she admired in them.

Her daughters were both attractive, bright-eyed, well-behaved children. I knew that, given the father's extensive addiction, it had been no small feat for the mother to provide for them. Her willingness to make the time for counseling despite her responsibilities as a working mom testified to her real concern for her family. Assuming that it would be easy for her to find something nice to say about her daughters, I was surprised when, instead of praising her daughters, she sat dumbly, unable to think of a single positive thing to say. It was a horrible moment.

Naturally I intervened and prompted her. "I don't suppose you could find anything nice to say about her eyes..." Her eldest had two of the largest and bluest eyes I'd ever seen. The mother began to talk about how beautiful her daughter's eyes were and, with more prodding, found something positive to say about her youngest.

This family had lived for so long in an atmosphere of such negativity and anxiety that they had lost their ability to see and affirm their own goodness. As a therapist working with families in crisis, I have found that helping people to discover and recover the goodness in themselves and others is critical to rebuilding a healthy family. This awareness of our goodness, the ability to name it and the practice of naming it, plays a vital role in the building of healthy families and in the prevention of family dysfunction.

Such a belief in the fundamental goodness of creation is central to the Judeo-Christian tradition. "In the beginning God created the heavens and the earth..." So begin the Hebrew scriptures. God creates light and "God saw that it was good" (Genesis 1:1, 4). As the creation story unfolds with each successive act of creation, this sentence—"And God saw that it was good"—is repeated again and again. The Hebrew word used here for "creation" refers exclusively to divine action. Human beings make things and form things, but only God creates something from nothing.[1] God creates good things and then takes the time to affirm the goodness of creation. God gives birth to creation and then blesses this creation.

Marriage calls us to be co-creators. The love that we give one another finds its source in God's love, an essentially creative love. God's love calls us to love others. God's life calls us to be life-givers in this world. A Christian marriage shares the life-giving love of God just as a fire by its nature radiates warmth. A marriage that exists only for the convenience and self-gratification of the couple is simply not a Christian marriage. I'm not referring only to bearing children; the creativity of our love can express itself in many ways as we care for others and care for our world.

Greater freedom of choice in fertility and the prevalence of two-career marriages mean that today's couples must make decisions about whether or not to use birth control, whether to have children and when to have them. Many couples desperately want children and cannot conceive. Some adopt children, but adoption is not the answer for every childless couple. Other couples delay having children because of concerns over career and finances. Some regret waiting; others are glad they did. Such decisions cannot be made lightly.

Though this book cannot fully address these issues, I acknowledge their difficulty and importance. I encourage couples to make such decisions in prayer and in a spirit of faith, creativity and generosity rather than a spirit of insecurity, doubt or self-gratification. I encourage couples who are unsure of their parental abilities or fearful of the economic and emotional responsibilities of parenthood, to spend some time with a healthy family. Talk honestly with parents who have faced the same insecurities successfully.

For many of us, however, much of the creativity and generosity of our love will find its expression in having and raising children. Children are often called blessings, and so they are. They express God's goodness. We did not create them, calling them into being out of nothingness, but through them we share in God's creative act. Like the Creator, we need to look on this creation and proclaim his or her goodness. This act of proclaiming the goodness of creation is at the heart of parenthood traditions.

Traditions of Pregnancy

Perhaps in no area of our society have there been more significant changes than in the role of women and the way of birth. Pregnancy has a profound effect on both partners, but most significantly transforms the woman. It is the woman whose body will undergo dramatic changes, the woman whose behavior most directly affects the infant's well-being, and the woman whose social and economic roles undergo radical changes. Because the woman's role in our society is most in flux as more women pursue careers and claim power in society, my comments will focus primarily on the woman's experience of pregnancy.

It is a peculiar adjunct to the improvement of women's status (her growing political and economic stature) that there should be a simultaneous devaluing of her role as mother. Today many perceive children as a threat rather than a help to the family economy. Pregnancy may be experienced as an interruption in a woman's career. I recall the discomfort I felt when acquaintances, on hearing I was pregnant, responded not with congratulations but with the question: "Do you want it?" It was assumed that, as a professional woman, I would not want the inconvenience of a child. I found this response nonsupportive. Mothers are often the scapegoats for society's ills. A woman is likely to find that while she is home with the infant she is perceived as less productive, less capable and less intelligent than she was while in the work force. These attitudes are often perpetrated not only by men but by other women.

I recall a Lamaze class I attended when I was pregnant with my daughter Elizabeth. Couples were asked if they had any special areas of concern. I expected questions about birthing techniques, medications, birth defects and the like. Instead, the majority of the women in the room expressed as their primary concern whether or not their figures would return to "normal" after birth. Normal was naturally defined as the figure depicted by our society's highly paid anorexic models. These women were anxious for their lives to get back to "normal" and to regain the appearance that won them the approval of society.

How sad it is that in our society women are more likely to be approved for their paychecks and their figures than for their role as mother. Furthermore, these young women were in for a rude awakening. Having a child profoundly changes one's life. Life doesn't ever get back to "normal"; nor should it.

The contemporary woman may be armed with more biological facts and medical aids than any woman in history, but in many ways she is less prepared and less supported in assuming her new role. Prior to the 19th century, childbirth in America was governed by age-old traditions, dominated by women and took place at home in the context of family and friends. By the end of the 19th century, childbirth was directed by the medical profession and had become an event dominated by men. In the 20th century, birth moved out of the home and into hospitals.

Although the medical profession can be thanked for an increase in a child's life expectancy today, its initial involvement in birth was fraught with problems. Such medical interventions as bloodletting, tobacco enemas and the use of opium for pain relief (which often slowed or halted contractions), the questionable use of chloroform and ether for anesthetics, often created problems which, in turn, required more medical interventions.[2] More problematic for us, however, is the fact that the medical approach in many ways removed birth from the normal cycle of life and pathologized it. In other words, the pregnant woman is treated not as a woman becoming a mother, but as a patient.

In Western medicine, the patient role has been a passive role. The doctors and medical staff become the "experts." Many women find it difficult to assert their own beliefs or express their needs in an environment where the doctor's schedule takes priority and where your weight gain and blood pressure, rather than your fears, hopes and dreams, are perceived as important. When the medical staff and the hospital became primary to birth, women lost much of the emotional and spiritual support that had accompanied home births, which had been guided by the women of the community.

Throughout human history, pregnancy was a dangerous time, and pregnant women were protected by myriad rules concerning what to eat and what to do. Some of the restrictions and prescriptions are clearly superstitious; others have their basis in common sense and experience. It is not hard to understand why an African woman is to avoid sick people while pregnant, or why an Egyptian husband takes care not to upset his wife for fear she will miscarry. The Tonawanda Seneca (a Native American tribe) believe that distress and unhappiness experienced by the pregnant mother make the baby unhappy, so every effort is taken to keep the mother happy and content.[3] In my grandmother's day, pregnant women were expected to listen to good music, read improving literature and avoid shock or stress as these could affect the baby's well-being. I recently met a 16-year-old at the hospital who was reading scripture to her yet unborn child. She explained that she had heard that the baby would love most whatever it heard while in the womb. I do not know if reading to a child in the womb will affect that child's literary tastes, but I have little doubt that as the scripture gave this young mother a sense of hope, it would ultimately benefit her child.

Pregnant women in New Guinea are told not to eat bandicoot, lest they die in labor, or frogs, lest labor be too quick, or eels, lest the baby be premature. (Most of us wouldn't need to be warned against such a diet.) In Guatemala, the mother-in-law guides the pregnancy. The pregnant woman must not go out when the sun is high or look at the full moon or a lunar eclipse, lest the baby be malformed. A Jamaican woman must not make too many preparations prior to the child's birth for fear that the child may be stillborn. This is similar to the English superstition that forbids a pregnant woman from buying a baby carriage before the baby's birth for fear that the baby will come to harm.[4] The pregnant woman was protected from frightening sights, which might harm her child, and if she craved a particular food she was to be given it at once.[5]

We may look askance at such superstitions; but these superstitious acts helped the pregnant woman deal with her fears. What does our culture do to help a pregnant woman deal with her fears—fears for her child, fears for her own health, fears of inadequacy, fears that her husband will not find her attractive, fears of financial difficulties? Many new mothers are teenage mothers and single mothers. More than half of the Americans living in poverty are single mothers and their children. For these women especially, pregnancy can be a lonely and stressful time. Their families often cannot provide the kind of support the woman needs.

It has been estimated that four out of five women go through reactive depression following childbirth.[6] For some women this is a brief period of the "blues," but for others it is a prolonged and difficult experience that significantly interferes with the well-being of both the mother and the child. The woman's experience during pregnancy affects her experience at childbirth. Furthermore, scientists have recently discovered what mothers have intuitively known for centuries: that the unborn child is sensitive to stimuli while still in the womb and that the relationship between parents and child begins before the child is born. Many psychologists now contend that pre-birth experience influences personality and aptitude. Too often we as a society or even a Christian community do little to support a woman during her pregnancy.

I believe that we need to consciously replace the traditions of superstition that once guided women through pregnancy with strong traditions of support. One of my favorite scriptures, the visitation of Mary to Elizabeth (after which we named our daughter, Elizabeth Mary), beautifully describes this support (read Luke 1:39-56). Mary, pregnant herself, goes to the support of her older cousin, further along with her pregnancy. I imagine these two women sharing a strengthening broth and a cozy chat together with a pillow wedged behind their lower backs and the little boys kicking away inside their wombs.

How many women need (and how few receive) this simple support. So many women work outside the home. So many are too busy. So many are separated from their mothers and grandmothers and aunts and older sisters. Even women who have family and friends ready to support them may be afraid to ask for help. Such fear seems to prevail among those, such as single mothers, who are most in need of support. Somehow many women have gotten the idea that they must "go it alone," as if pregnancy and birth were some sort of macho event in which women demonstrate their independence and internal fortitude. Now I come from pioneer stock and I'm all for stiff upper lips when necessary, but I agree that it takes a village to raise a child. As Christians we need to support others and to be open to support for ourselves. The village needs to reach out to the pregnant woman and offer her the support she may hesitate to request.

The father is a primary support for the pregnant woman, and many fathers today take a more active role in birth and its preparations. Single mothers may wish to choose a birthing companion to provide them with support. Birthing classes provide the support of peers and instructors sympathetic to new mothers' (and fathers') needs. This atmosphere is usually more personal and supportive than the doctor's office.

Many women are choosing to use a *doula* for support during pregnancy and birth. The doula is a woman trained to provide emotional support and to help increase the physical comfort and well-being of a woman during pregnancy and birth. It should come as no surprise to Christians that tending to our spiritual health affects our physical health. Scientific studies indicate that this support reduces the number of Cesarean sections, shortens labor and decreases the use of anesthesia and forceps. Newborns are likely to be healthier when moms receive the support they need.[7]

Today's pregnant woman needs affirmation. She needs to be told that her state is natural and good. The practice in some churches of having a few Sundays a year when the community invites its pregnant women to come forward for a special blessing is a wonderful way to help a woman feel the support of the Christian community. At our church, women are invited to come forward for a special prayer and blessing and are given a rose and a prayer card. This not only gives these woman an opportunity to feel affirmed, but also encourages the community to reach out to these women, expressing support at other church gatherings.

Many cultures bless the parents-to-be after the pregnancy is confirmed and several times during the pregnancy. The blessing may be given by a priest, deacon, minister, friend or family member. Traditionally, blessings are often given by the parents of the parents-to-be. The blessing may be said before saying grace at a family meal. Scripture may be read (for example, Psalm 128) and a simple prayer said.[8] The person giving the blessing may wish to place his or her hands on the parents' heads. Verbal or silent prayers can also be said by other family members and friends (as each places his or her hands on the heads of the new parents), concluding with the Our Father or with a benediction.

Some traditions of pregnancy link extended families to each other. In Sumatra, in the fifth month, the woman's mother gives rice cakes and a gift of money to the man's mother. In the seventh month, the man's mother brings rice, spices, soap, powder and a new sarong to the expectant mother.[9] I am not aware of a similar tradition in our culture, but I think we might consider creating one. As I have stated before, extended family ties are often nonexistent or weakened in our highly mobile society. Yet the extended family is a key source of support and guidance for young parents.

Young couples need to know that both sides of their families are united in support behind them. Where there have been strained or difficult relationships within a family, as in the case of divorce or in blended families, an act of solidarity on the part of the family can provide the young couple with much-needed emotional support. This might be done by one set of future grandparents inviting the other set of future grandparents out to dinner to toast the future grandchild. When no extended family is present, close neighbors and friends might assume this role, creating get-togethers where they can celebrate the upcoming birth.

Nesting seems to be a biological urge among women in the last trimester and gives rise to traditions involving preparing the child's sleeping area and clothing and blessing the child's room or crib. Having friends over to help with some of these preparations can provide pragmatic support as the birth approaches. Families and friends often celebrate with the expectant woman at showers. These are intimate parties, usually given in the last trimester, where baby presents are given, experiences shared and good wishes extended.

Pregnancy and Prayer

Because pregnancy is such a life-changing event, it is particularly important to give your spiritual life the opportunity to grow at this time. If you do not already have a special space that belongs to you, this is a good time to create one. It does not need to be a separate room, but might be a corner of a room set aside for you. My corner has a comfortable rocking chair, a small shelf for my journal, favorite books and objects I use in meditation and reflection (such as my rosary, a votive candle and various keepsakes). Your children will make their presence felt in every corner of your life; it can be helpful to have your own space set aside where you can go for your own nurturing. The nurturer needs nurturing, and when we take on the responsibilities of parenthood, it is often easy to neglect our own needs. Attention to your own spiritual needs will enable you to be more giving and generous with your spouse and children. Set aside a space and time for personal reflection and prayer.

Develop prayer traditions now that help you become quiet and calm and that will last through the disruptions of early parenting. Many of the traditions in the chapter on single life will be useful now, particularly the breathing prayers and invocations. There are numerous resources available to help us in our prayer and reflection. Spend some time looking over the prayer books and spiritual readings available in your local bookstores or at your library. There are many scriptural passages one might meditate on at this time, such as Psalm 131, where the psalmist seeks to be as calm in God's presence as a child on its mother's lap; Psalm 136, which praises our Creator's steadfast love; or Psalm 139, in which the psalmist reflects on God's involvement in his life since his days in his mother's womb. You might find Dr. Verny and Pamela Weintraub's book, *Nurturing the Unborn Child*, a good resource for exercises that can be incorporated into your prayer life.[10]

In the Christian tradition, God is often portrayed as masculine. But pregnancy, when a woman prepares for her parental role, is a good time to reflect on God as mother and to explore the feminine aspects of God in our tradition. In the Hebrew scriptures, God is depicted as a mother eagle (Deuteronomy 32:11). The Hebrew word for God's mercy, *rahamim*, derives from the word for womb, *rehem*. The words "merciful father," therefore, could be translated "motherly father." The Hebrew word for wisdom is feminine and *shekhinah*, the word for God that expresses God's presence on earth, is also feminine. Both the gospels of Matthew and Luke (Matthew 23:37; Luke 13:34) describe God as a mother hen, a delightful image that, surprisingly, was used by St. Anselm in his ontological proof of God's existence.[11]

Pregnancy also serves as an excellent time to develop your relationship with Mary. This may be done simply by meditating on her life events or by asking her for support during pregnancy. As Christians, we believe in eternal life and the communion of saints. When we look to the saints as models for our own behavior or speak to them from the sincerity of our hearts, we practice this faith and provide ourselves with a support system that extends far beyond the confines of our own particular community.

Praying the rosary continues to be a source of great comfort and inspiration for many Christians. The repetitive nature of the rosary and the physical fingering of the beads is calming to mind and body and can help a person enter into a prayerful state. It is traditional to begin with the Apostles' Creed, followed by the Lord's Prayer, three Hail Marys and then to pray each of five decades (made up of ten Hail Marys preceded by the Lord's Prayer and followed by the Glory to the Father). The rosary concludes with Hail Holy Queen.

You can pray the five decades while reflecting on certain mysteries. The Joyful Mysteries may have special importance for the pregnant woman as they reflect on Mary's pregnancy and motherhood. They include the Annunciation (Luke 1:30-33), the Visitation (Luke 1:39-45), the Nativity (Luke 2:4-7), the Presentation (Luke 2:22-38) and the Finding of Jesus in the Temple (Luke 2:41-52). There are numerous variations on the rosary (the seven dolors, the five wounds, and the scriptural rosary, to name a few). You may wish to adapt the rosary to your personal prayer needs. Rosary prayers can be found in many different resources at a variety of bookstores.

A tradition among many of my African American friends is to have a prayer partner or prayer sister. This person, although not biologically related, is often introduced simply as one's sister, and visits the mother to pray with her and for her before, during and after the birth. The prayer sister is usually a person of strong faith and practical experience who is a wonderful resource for the young parents.

Good spiritual preparation for parenting is one of the best ways to honor both your needs and the needs of your child. The arrival of your first child will change your life forever. Children are people. They are not short adults. They are not extensions of our own personalities. They are not dolls or playthings. Children are people, and they start out being people while they are still in the womb. Our relationship with our children begins during pregnancy. Pregnancy is more than a time of preparation; it is a time of relationship. It is the beginning of your relationship with your new child and the beginning of radical changes in all your other relationships.

You and your spouse will need to make significant changes in your lives. Many couples move during pregnancy or not long after their first child is born. Most new parents will have less private time together and less sleep (at least for awhile). You will have financial decisions to make. And you will be taking on a role, awesome in its importance, that you may well feel inadequate to fulfill. As you prepare for these changes in your life, as you begin this new relationship, give yourself time, space and support. Nourish the nurturer. If you were planting a new tree in your yard, you would prepare the soil. Now is the time to prepare the spiritual soil in which you will plant this new little life.

Traditions of Birth

The advent of hospital births and the over-reliance on the medical profession to meet the needs of mother and child not only had an impact on the actual birth, but a significant effect on child care as well. The radical changes in birth, nursing and early child care may be among the most significant and least understood phenomena of our century. Certainly these changes have had a profound impact on the spiritual experience of mothers and children. Any negative impact is not the fault of the medical profession, but of an entire society that, in the face of remarkable changes, neglected basic emotional and spiritual needs. The Christian church must accept some responsibility for this.

I was disturbed when I began researching this book to find, for example, that primary resources, such as Christian encyclopedias, contained a few skimpy paragraphs on birth, but numerous pages on birth control. This epitomizes the way in which the church has too often dealt with the problems that have arisen as the result of the Industrial Revolution and 20th-century technology. The church tends to become embroiled in controversy, defending its teachings. Though this may on occasion be necessary and valuable, I think more effort needs to be directed at articulating and supporting that which may not be controversial but is nonetheless essential. In other words, the church should have more to say (and with greater energy) about the spiritual importance of birth than about birth control.

Birth is a profoundly spiritual experience. Like most true spiritual experiences, it isn't what we expect a spiritual experience to be. It's messy, it's painful, it's not something we can control; and yet most parents will tell you, there is no experience to match it in power, beauty and importance. If you value life you will be profoundly moved by birth. It challenges us, opens us up, changes us. And it brings into the world a new being, a new creation.

In the Judeo-Christian tradition, the birth of a child is a gift of God and a time of rejoicing for parents, extended family and the community. The injunction to "be fruitful and multiply" (Genesis 1:28) is considered a commandment, or *mitzvah*, in the Bible, a way to honor and own our part of the covenental relationship between God and the people of God.

There are many folk customs surrounding birth, but many of these fell by the wayside with the decrease in home births and the dominance of the medical profession. Many of these traditions were superstitious in origin, but others had their foundation in practical care and comfort of mother and child. In Sephardic tradition, for example, certain scriptural passages were recited while a woman was in labor. These might have included Genesis 21:1-8, 1 Samuel 1 or Psalm 20. A Jewish woman having a difficult labor might have had the keys to the synagogue placed in her hands or a band of a Torah scroll placed on her.[12] Talismans were sometimes hung about the room. Through these concrete ways a woman was both comforted and strengthened to keep her focus during the difficult and often life-threatening experience of childbirth.

Today a Christian mother might cling to a rosary, cross or medal. The presence of such symbols need not be superstitious or magical, but can be simple ways of helping the woman stay focused on the meaning of her birthing experience. The supportive presence of her husband or birthing companion can provide comfort and help her to hold onto hope when labor is difficult. Many women today choose either not to use anesthetics, or to use limited amounts, and to use birthing methods such as Lamaze to help with pain. This "awake and aware" approach to childbirth has numerous health benefits for mother and child. The alert woman can benefit from the use of sacramentals and the presence of supportive people in the birthing process.

I vividly remember the births of my two girls as among the most powerful and grace-filled moments of my life, but I readily admit that it was not easy to keep focused. Pain management is an issue, of course, but for me, I needed help not just in dealing with pain, but in dealing with the psychological and spiritual impact of the experience. Birth can thrust you into a psychological state that is at once powerful and unfamiliar. Transition, that final intense moment in the birthing process, is, for many women, an experience that is simply beyond normal experience. I have heard some mothers describe it as a state of altered consciousness. When I reached this point in our daughter Teresa's birth, I felt that the only thing keeping me going was the simple fact that it was too late to stop. It wasn't just a matter of pain; it was as if the experience was too immense for me to contain. My husband, sensing my altered state of mind, grabbed the tiny baby T-shirt laid out on the crib next to my bed, held it in front of my face and cried, "There is a baby!" I'd lost sight of the baby in the intensity of the experience, but the sight of that T-shirt and my husband's words refocused me.

Be creative in integrating your religious beliefs into your birthing experience. If you are using Lamaze, you might wish to incorporate breathing prayers (see chapter 1) into your meditations. These meditations can not only help in pain management, but will help open you to the presence of God. Men and women preparing for childbirth pack all sorts of things (bags of ice, lollipops, washcloths, camera, phone numbers) to prepare for birthing. Spend a moment thinking about what you will need spiritually and discuss this with your spouse. One woman I know bought a small cross to hold during labor. She saved the cross and gave it to her child at the time of the child's first communion. Some people pay particular attention to the clothing in which they will first dress the newborn and the receiving blanket in which they will wrap the child.

In early America, women gave birth at home where they could move about at will and give birth in any position that suited them. When labor began, the women assisting in the birth would brew soothing teas. Amber, saffron, ground cumin seed, sage or comfrey were used to ease the woman through dilation. Myrrh might be used to hasten delivery and a mint syrup to help with nausea. A fern paste was used to keep the perineum pliant, and after birth a woman might drink a bayberry tea if she was bleeding too much or betony root if she seemed hysterical. The baby and mother were cleaned and wrapped in soft blankets for warmth and comfort. Black midwives, called "grannies," supervised birth among both black and white women in the South, and were known for their ability in helping with both spiritual and medical concerns.[13]

Without in any way denying the immense benefits of contemporary medicine, I think we have too readily let go of some of the birthing traditions of support and comfort. This may, in part, account for the postpartum reactive depression experienced by so many women. Fortunately, an appreciation of the need for emotional and spiritual support in addition to medical expertise is growing. Many birthing centers now encourage women to move about more freely, to brew a soothing tea and to surround themselves with supportive people. The use of midwives has increased in recent years, and with it, more attention to the spiritual and emotional needs of the mother. As women are often in the hospital only briefly nowadays, the home once again becomes a place to recuperate from the excitement and stress of birth.

As you prepare for birth, be proactive in arranging for the support you will need after birth. Encourage a close friend or relative to stay with you the first few days or week. If possible, plan on doing nothing but caring for your baby. Surround yourself with comfortable pillows, comforting people, nourishing food, relaxing music, a good book. Here is an herbal tea that makes a comforting drink for after birth. (For a guide to making culinary and medicinal teas, consult *Rodale's Illustrated Encyclopedia of Herbs*, Claire Kowalchik and William H. Hylton, eds. [Emmaus, PA: Rodale Press, 1987], 484–486.)

Mint Herbal Tea

Fill a teapot with hot water from the tap. Heat 1 quart water in kettle. When water boils, pour out hot water in teapot, put 2 ounces dried herbs in brewing basket (or use tea bags). You might use dill seed (to increase milk), chamomile (to soothe and relax), and/or a slice of ginger (to give energy, soothe indigestion and relieve cramping). Put brewing basket and 6–10 fresh mint leaves in pot. Fill teapot with boiling water, cover with cozy and let steep 10 minutes. Pour into small heavy glasses or teacups. Add sugar or honey to taste.

My sister-in-law had such speedy deliveries that she (and her mother) rarely made it to the hospital on time. Several of the children in their family were born in taxis and elevators. Not surprisingly she opted for home birth, at which my brother and a midwife assisted. She waxes eloquent on the benefits of the herbal bath she was given not long after birth. So relaxing, so refreshing, she tells me. I, on the other hand, lay covered with blood in my hospital bed from 12:30 a.m., when Teresa was delivered, until 10 a.m., when someone came in to help me clean myself up. The medical profession is quite naturally more concerned with the safe delivery of the child than with the emotional and spiritual needs of mother and child. As Christians, we need to be concerned with both.

Soothing Herbal Bath

Wrap dried herbs in cheesecloth or muslin and hang from the faucet while filling the tub. To soothe and relax, use valerian, chamomile flowers, lemon balm and rose flowers.

Most parents like to touch and examine their newborn, counting fingers and toes, gazing in wonder at this new little being. This is a natural time for prayers of gratitude and blessing. Bless each finger as you count it. Hold your baby and your spouse's hand and say a prayer of thanksgiving, ask God to guide you as parents, speak the needs and desires of your heart. One of the oldest prayers used at the time of birth comes from the Jewish tradition: "Blessed is the Lord our God, Ruler of the universe for giving us life, for sustaining us, and for enabling us to reach this joyous occasion." It is traditional among some Christians to recite the Lord's Prayer at the birth. If you have other children, have your other children join you to meet the baby and say prayers of thanksgiving. It is traditional in some families for the other children to bring gifts for the newborn and for the parents to have gifts ready for the newborn to give his or her new siblings. This both celebrates the birth and can help alleviate some of the anxiety and jealousy other children sometimes experience.

Another lovely tradition for after birth is widely practiced in India, where it is customary to massage the baby. If you have a hospital birth, you might wish to give your baby a massage to relax the child when you return home. Use pure olive oil or baby oil. Place a towel under the baby. Be gentle and loving. (Consult Frederick Leboyay's *Loving Hands: The Traditional Art of Baby Massaging* [New York: Knopf, 1976].) There is no reason why the baby should be the only one to get a massage. Mom and Dad can express their affection for one another by giving each other massages. If you have other children, give them massages too. I still give my children massages when they are stressed or just need a little loving. Play soothing music. Light a fire in the fireplace. It is amazing how relaxing and comforting touch can be. Rocking your child and singing lullabies is another tradition of comfort important after birth. Young siblings may want to be rocked and sung to now, even if they have gotten "too old" for such things. Birth is exciting and joyful but it is also tiring and stressful. We all need reassurance, comfort and a little peace and quiet.

Celebrating Birth

Most parents begin announcing the birth while still at the hospital with calls to friends and relatives, who will, in turn, call other friends and relatives. Many parents will also send out birth announcements. Let older children help with these important phone calls, card making and letter sending.

Many Chinese Americans have a "red egg" party when the child is one month old. Red eggs are given at a dinner party as a thank-you to friends and family who have given gifts to the baby and supported the parents through the birth. Some families, instead of having a dinner party, give thank-you bags. Two eggs, hard-boiled and dyed red, two oranges, sweet pickled ginger and Chinese roast pork are put into paper bags. These bags are then delivered to family and friends as a thank-you.

In Jewish tradition it is considered a *mitzvah* to make a gift of *tzedakah* (charity) in honor of one's child at the time of birth. This beautiful tradition reminds us that the blessings we receive from God are not for ourselves alone, but need to be blessings for the world beyond us. It is particularly appropriate to honor one's child by making a gift to one's church, a religious school, or some other organization that supports the values you wish your child to grow up with.

Many birth traditions call to mind God's parental care for the child. A Mexican tradition, originally from the Huichol people, which has found its way into Christian practice, is the making of "God's eyes," or *tsikuri*, at the time of a child's birth. Strands of brightly colored wool are stretched over a wooden cross to form a diamond of color. Huichol fathers would make these on the birth of their children, dedicating them to the deities. Two more were made when the child was 2 years old and five more made on the child's fifth birthday.[14] In Christian usage, the God's eye is a symbol of God's faithful care of children. The cross on which the wool is wound reminds us of the cross of Jesus.

Today many people have pictures or figurines depicting guardian angels in the newborn's room. Guardian angels are a tradition of long standing. The Talmud tells us that every Jew is assigned eleven thousand guardian angels at birth and the Christian Church teaches, in the words of St. Basil, "Beside each believer stands an angel as protector and shepherd, leading him to life."[15] I recall as a child looking up at the guardian angel picture hung above my bed and drawing comfort from it. One of my daughters has a wooden angel my mother sent from Barcelona hanging above the door to her room, and the other has a wooden plaque with the word *shalom*. In the Christian tradition, daisies symbolize innocence, so daisies are sometimes given to decorate the newborn's room or used to decorate the infant's clothing. If the child has been named after an admired relative or saint, you may wish to hang a picture of this person. These images and meaningful decorations help create an environment of peace, grace and care.

The symbol of the tree of life is used to celebrate birth in many cultures. An ancient Jewish tradition found in the Talmud[16] is to celebrate a child's birth by planting a tree. Parents plant cedars for boys and pines for girls. Child and tree grow together, and when the child attains adulthood the tree is cut down and the branches are used to make the bridal canopy.

The tradition of planting a tree has found its way into Christian practice, although I am not aware of a tradition that makes use of the tree. Certainly one could use the boughs for decoration at one's wedding or have a Welsh wedding spoon carved from the wood. You might plant an evergreen and make an Advent wreath from its cones.

In our society we are so rarely connected with the products we use or the food we eat. We rarely see the trees from which our furniture and homes are made or the plants and the animals from which our daily food and milk come; but it can be important to experience these connections at times. Planting a tree at your child's birth and having something of significance made from that tree can help one to experience how our lives are intimately connected to the creation that surrounds us.

Your child's birth is a good time to make a family tree, including the latest arrival. A family tree can take many forms. You might pick a wall for your family gallery and hang pictures of the family, or write out the family tree on a piece of drawing paper, and frame it. If you are artistic, try drawing a tree and let the leaves contain the family names. Include the newborn's name, siblings, parents, grandparents and great-grandparents.

The family tree can be especially important for blended and divorced families as a concrete way of affirming the family's connectedness. I remember one time when I asked a divorced mother and her child to draw pictures of their family. She drew herself and her child. Her child drew himself, his mother, his father, his father's girlfriend, her child and their three dogs. It was important for this mother to understand and acknowledge that her child's view of family was different from her own. Whatever divisions and conflicts a family has experienced, they are the child's roots and a sense of their connection can be important to the child's identity.

I would not shy away from making a family tree if you are adopting your child. Your family is your child's psycho-social and spiritual roots, and your child is a necessary and essential part of your family. In an open adoption you will have information about the birth parents and this can be included in the family tree. But what if you have no information? There is a lovely Jewish tradition in which an adopted child is named "the son or daughter of Abraham our father and Sarah our mother." Abraham and Sarah are the spiritual parents of Jews and Christians alike. There is a beautiful *midrash* in which we are told that Abraham and Sarah's tent was open on four sides so that guests could enter from all directions.[17] A family who adopts opens the doors of their home on all sides, inviting others to enter. If you cannot put the biological names of your child's ancestors on the family tree, why not put the names of his or her spiritual ancestors, Abraham and Sarah? In this way you acknowledge your child's larger heritage. You could keep your family tree in a photo album, including photos and family stories.

Many people have a tradition of keeping a large family Bible in which births are recorded in the back. This family Bible has a place of honor in the home and is read from on holidays and for special family events. Many people begin a baby book at the time of baby's birth, and some baby books have a place for a family tree. The baby book and family trees are popular with children as they grow up, especially when they include stories about themselves and the people they love. Children want to know where they come from and who they come from. Parents may wish to write a letter to or a blessing for their newborn to include with the family tree. A growing child will read and reread a parent's simple heartfelt message.

Another early American tradition that is enjoying a revival is the making of a special crib quilt. Wrapping baby up in womb-like warmth is a tradition as old as our species. Jesus was wrapped in swaddling clothes, bands of cloth wrapped about the infant to restrict movement and help the baby retain heat. Children often become attached to the comforting receiving blanket, carrying its tattered remnants into their toddler years (and sometimes to college). It is not surprising then that parents should try to make this little "security" blanket something special.

Receiving blankets are important to our family. We had three lovely blankets: a soft blanket my grandmother had knitted in which we wrapped our babies when they were first born, a crib quilt made by my mother in which we wrapped our babies when they went home from the hospital, and a lovely wool blanket woven by my mother-in-law in which we wrapped the children at the time of their baptism.

A crib quilt can be made as simply or elaborately as one wants, but it should be made from a soft, washable and durable material that is not readily flammable (avoid polyesters that melt into hot liquid if burned). After our children outgrew the crib quilt, I put it away in the cedar chest. It didn't stay there long. Every Christmas Eve we have a tree-blessing ceremony. It begins with a procession, carrying the candles from the Advent wreath, and continues with songs, prayers, scripture and the ritual of the youngest child in the household placing baby Jesus (a baby doll) in a wooden cradle. Then the tree lights are lit. When they were still quite little, the children, preparing baby Jesus for this event, went to the cedar chest and took out the crib quilt, carefully wrapping the baby in it. Our children are now teenagers but every Christmas Eve, baby Jesus is still carefully wrapped in the little crib quilt that once covered them and is placed in the wooden crib beneath the tree. Here are directions for a simple pieced quilt.

Crib Quilt

For a quilt 30 by 45 inches, you will need:
   $3/_8$ yards each of five different print fabrics (45 inches in width)
      that look well together
   $3/_4$ yard of matching gingham
   1 $3/_8$ yards flannel and thread to match

Preshrink and press fabric.

Using a yardstick, measure, mark and cut three strips 3 $1/_2$ inches wide out of each of the print fabrics. Divide strips into three groups and arrange each group. With right sides together, stitch strips of each group together, making a $1/_4$-inch seam. Press seams to one side. You should have three rectangles. Measure and mark lines 3 $1/_2$ inches apart perpendicular to seams. Cut on lines. Lay out strips to make a 30 by 45 inch quilt. Stitch together five block rows (with $1/_4$-inch seam allowance), pressing seams in one direction until you have your quilt top pieced together.

Cut gingham in strips 3 inches wide, sewing strips together at ends to make one long strip for ruffle. Fold in half, wrong sides together, press. Gather raw edges and pin to quilt top, right sides together, easing gathers to fit. Stitch.

Cut batting slightly larger than 30 by 45 inches. Lay batting on floor. Over it place felt backing right side up and quilt top right side down. Pin layers together and trim excess batting. Stitch together leaving one short edge open. Turn right side out, pin together and machine quilt. Hand stitch open end together. Decorate by tacking on small bows of matching ribbon if desired.

In many families an aunt or grandparent makes the child's Christmas stocking at the time of the child's birth. These can be personal, beautiful and a lifetime source of joy. In my family, our stockings were small and made of velveteen beautifully appliquéed by my aunt with an assortment of colorful figures and gold cording. My husband's grandmother knit huge stockings for them out of colored wool. Their names were knit into the design. My mother-in-law wove a stocking for my eldest daughter that opens up into a banner for her birthday, and my sister-in-law knit a beautiful stocking for our youngest. Although my husband and I no longer have our stockings filled, the children insist that we still hang them up each year for decoration.

Naming Traditions

Names have a special significance in the Judeo-Christian tradition. According to one Jewish teaching, every person has three names: the name given by the parents, the name others call them by, and the name that they make for themselves.[18] The names we give our children reflect our beliefs, our dreams and often the heritage we pass on to our children. As these names become part of our child's identity, they must be meaningful. You may wish to choose a name from scripture, a saint's name, or the name of a religious or spiritual figure whom you admire.

The custom of giving children the names of saints dates from the first century and is customary in many cultures. Prior to the advent of the Normans, however, saints' names were not used by Irish Christians, who would have considered it irreverent to assume a holy name. Some Irish clans called themselves the servants (*gil, mal*) of our Lord and the saints (e.g., Gilpatrick and Gilmary). Many cultures consider it irreverent to use the name *Jesus*; however, Spanish-speaking cultures are an exception. Hispanic cultures often use not only Mary's names but her attributes: Dolores (Our Lady of Sorrows), Stella (Star of the Sea), Consuela

(Our Lady of Good Counsel). Syrians and Chaldeans traditionally used Mary's name (Miriam) and attributes such as beauty (Jamala) and purity (Afifa).[19]

You may wish to pick the name of an admired historical figure or of a loved and honored relative. You may choose a name because of its meaning. Native American parents often named their children for qualities observed in nature that they believed the child would possess. Early American Protestants were often named for virtues their parents hoped they would have. This was true in my family. If I had been named after my grandmother and my great-grandmother, I would have had to bear the burden of Constance Patience!

Many families name children after grandparents. In one Eastern European tradition, parents name children after deceased relatives. Many Orthodox Christians name a child after an orthodox saint, an important feast day, a biblical event or Christian symbol, such as the cross (*stavros*). In Greece, the child is often called "baby" until he or she is baptized.[20] Some parents create names for their children out of combinations of people's names. For example, one of my African American friends chose the name Lavanna Dakota. Lavanna was a combination of her name, Vanetta, her mother's name, Anna, and her husband's name, Larry. Dakota was the name of her prayer sister.

For centuries, people straddling cultures have given names that represent both cultures in which they live. Biblical examples of this practice include Esther/ Hadassah (Esther 2:7) and Daniel/Belteshazzar (Daniel 1:7). This tradition recognizes the need to retain a link to one's past while forging a link to one's future. For our children we chose names that had spiritual, familial and ethnic significance. Teresa Helen is named after Teresa of Avila, but also for my mother, grandmother and sisters-in-law. Our daughter Elizabeth Mary is named after the Visitation, and also after her mother, great-grandmother and great-great grandmother. Both of their names are easily translated into Irish, Trassa Eileen and Eilish Moira. The Irish forms of their names are occasionally used, especially when we need to distinguish between the three Teresas in our family (called in Irish, Trassa-Mor, Trassa-Beag and Trassa-Ruha, or big, little and red Teresa).

Usually parents choose the child's name, but not always. In one Greek Orthodox tradition, the godparent chooses the name. In some villages in Greece, the parents wait at home while the godparent presents the child for baptism. Children gather in the narthex, waiting to hear the godparent say the child's name, then hurry to the parents' house to tell them. The parents give money or a gift to the first child to deliver this important piece of news. The parents then go to the church to receive the newly baptized child. A version of this tradition practiced by some

Greek Americans calls for the parents to wait outside the church and give a coin to the first child to tell the baby's name.[21]

If you have named your child after a particular relative or religious figure, you may wish to have a picture of this person in your child's room and an explanation of why you chose the name in the baby book. Or you can purchase or make a plaque or wall hanging that gives the child's name and its meaning.

Let There Be Milk

Egyptians attempted feeding infants from feeding vessels as long ago as 2500 B.C. Egyptian etchings and Greek myths refer to the practice of suckling animals, and the use of wet nurses was common among wealthy Romans and Egyptians. The vast majority of women throughout history, however, have breast-fed their young, until the 20th century.

During the Industrial Revolution, as more families became fragmented, more women were forced into the labor market. The idea of the working woman wasn't anything new. Women had been gathering food, tending farms, caring for live-stock and working within the home for centuries. What was new was the separation of the working mother from her child. Children were taken with mothers into the fields, but not into the factories. Around 1600, women first began using pap gruel (milk with bread, rice or flour) to feed their children while they went off to work. By 1800, seven out of eight artificially-fed children died, and foundling hospitals had a mortality rate of 80 percent or higher. In colonial America, when the milk of cows and goats was used for feeding, the mortality rate of infants jumped from 50 percent to 65 percent.

The most dramatic changes in breast-feeding occurred in the 20th century. In 1930, more than 70 percent of first-born infants were nursed. By the 1960s this had declined to 18 percent. And yet there was no enforceable law regarding infant formula until the Infant Formula Act was passed by Congress in 1980. Even with better regulations, formula has proven to be less healthy for children than mother's milk. Further, formulas are susceptible to misuse. Many Hispanic and Vietnamese infants were hospitalized after their caregivers, unable to read the English instructions, gave them full-strength formula.[22]

When formula, rather than mother's milk, became the sustenance of choice in the 20th century, millions of women were told that they couldn't or shouldn't nurse their own children. Many of today's women continue to carry burdens of poor self-confidence and ignorance imposed on their mothering by this approach. Women and children were often separated at birth, the most intense time for bonding. Parents were encouraged to schedule feedings (often at four-hour intervals) and naps for their children. This radically changed the way child care had been practiced, and it had a significant effect on generations of children and their parents. Research has since shown that formula does not provide the health benefits of the mother's milk. Breast milk is more easily digestible, superior nutritionally and contains antibodies that protect against infection. Nursing speeds the return of the uterus to normal, stimulates the release of hormones that delay ovulation and menstruation for several months and helps the mother's emotional state.

The health factor, however, may be the least significant problem posed by the devaluing of nursing. Parents were taught to listen to outside authorities and to trust theories rather than their own beliefs, intuitions and assessment of their children's needs. The doctor's schedule, rather than the child's cry of hunger, determined when the child would be fed. Psychological theories, rather than parental observations, values and intuitions about their child's behavior, determined parental response. This meant that parenting became less individualized; parents were discouraged from tuning into their children's cues and further discouraged from valuing their own beliefs and instincts. Infants were taught from birth that the world was unresponsive to their needs unless they could fit their needs into the world's schedule. This is an inherently anti-spiritual approach to life in which mechanical regimens rather than relational responsiveness are valued. I believe it may be many generations before we will fully understand the impact this movement had on childbearing in our culture.

Certainly some women are unable to nurse for physical or emotional reasons. Does this mean they are inferior mothers or that their children won't turn out well? Of course not. It means that each mother and child must have their needs respected. The number of women unable to nurse successfully is in fact a small percentage of women. Many women who think they can't nurse, can if given support. Parents need to be supported in giving their children the very best they have to offer, physically, emotionally and spiritually. This support needs to come from family, friends and medical professionals.

What is the father's role in nursing? My own experience leads me to say that the father's role in nursing is vital. In fact, so important is this role that I strongly encourage single moms to find someone to provide this support. What does the father do? When I was nursing, my husband ran interference. He fended off negative influences that could create anxiety and insecurity in me. Our society has been so negative about nursing for so long that these negative influences prevail. The father is also the relief pitcher. Caring for an infant is an overwhelming full-time job, especially in the first few months after birth. No matter how much you love your child, you will become cranky or anxious or depressed if you go too long without a break. If mom is at home with the child, the father, even though he has had a long hard day at work, is likely to be able to approach the baby with a fresh, energetic, fun-filled attitude that mom is not going to have.

Babies pick up on our moods quickly and respond accordingly. The more tired and stressed the parents, the more irritable the child. Mothers who work outside the home have a tough job and need immense amounts of support and understanding. If they don't get this from their spouses they are unlikely to get it at all. Parents will find that they have different parenting gifts. It is easy for a father to think that baby only wants mom because mom has milk, but babies want far more of our lives than milk. They want fun and the chance to explore and constant comfort. Many nursing moms report that fathers are often better at getting babies to fall asleep. Any parent of an infant will tell you that getting baby to sleep is of paramount importance. Some fathers feel that they have a diminished role while the child is nursing. This is far from true. They simply have a less visible role, a state many men will be unaccustomed to. Women, I think, are more accustomed to taking invisible roles in our culture.

The way in which we approach breast-feeding is strongly influenced by our culture. In France, a woman may go topless on a beach but will cover herself carefully while nursing. Whereas in Saudi Arabia, a heavily veiled woman may unselfconsciously bare her breast to nurse her child in public. In the Dominican Republic, the child is put to the breast whenever he or she cries, and in New Guinea, a mother may not only nurse her own children but a neighbor's child should the need arise (due to death or sickness).[23]

I find it interesting that in the United States, where nakedness is commonplace on television and in movies, many people are embarrassed or offended by a woman discreetly nursing in public. I recall singing an anthem in a church choir in which the original words (from a Christina Rosetti poem) "a breast full of milk" had been changed to "a heart full of mirth" as people thought the word *breast* might be offensive. The La Leche League found that the word *breast* got their meeting notices banned from newspapers, so they named their group after the Spanish word for milk. In our culture, breasts are sexualized, and we are, in spite of our promiscuity (or perhaps because of it), rather prudish.

Because nursing has been less common in our culture in the last few decades, we have lost touch with some of the traditions and experiential wisdom that guided women through the centuries. The La Leche League has probably done more than any other group to right some of these wrongs. This group began with seven Catholic women who wanted to breast-feed their children. They got together in Mary White's Franklin Park living room to talk and drink coffee. They believed that a woman should listen to her body, a concept popular now but not in 1956. Just as birth had become a medical event and the mother a patient, child feeding had become a medical matter, and big business. These women felt that feeding a baby was a maternal matter. They began to share their experience, supporting each other. Within a few years they were getting inquiries from women all over the world. I believe that their spirituality had a great deal to do with their ability to look within themselves for what was right for them and for their children, giving them the courage to reach out to each other and act in accordance with their beliefs, albeit contrary to society.

For nursing to be a fulfilling experience for mother and child, the mother needs to be able to look at her body and bless it. She needs to be able to say: my breasts are good, and my milk is good. She needs other people in her life who will bless her. She needs a husband who is mature enough to say: "While you are caring for our child I will care for you" and not, "Why aren't you taking care of me?"

In cultures where breast-feeding is practiced "on demand," that is, whenever the child indicates he or she is hungry, there are traditional wraps used to carry the child close to the mother's breast. A Zambian infant is secured to the mother twenty-four hours after delivery by a long piece of cloth. In Bolivia, a strong cotton fabric called *aguawo* is folded into a baby carrier. Mexican women use a shawl called a *rebozo*.[24] In this way the child is kept comforted and secure, can nurse easily, and is offered many opportunities for stimulation as he or she is carried about.

Many nursing traditions involve obtaining a good milk supply. Navajo women believed that drinking a broth made from blue corn meal increased the milk supply, and Ojibwa Indian mothers ate wild rice, lake trout and white fish. Filipino women drink a soup made with marangay leaves and papaya, and Chinese women use herbs in their food and teas to provide a balance of yin and yang. In Mexico, anise and cotton seed were used to increase milk supply. In Japan, women are given figurines or pictures of women with full breasts to encourage an increase in their milk. Some temples give the woman a votive picture called an *ema*. The mother prays for sufficient milk, and if her prayer is answered she writes her name and age on the plaque and dedicates it to the temple. Hispanic women may pray to Nuester Senora de la Leche y Bueno Paro (Our Lady of Happy Delivery and Plentiful Milk).[25]

The quantity or quality of milk is often less of a problem than a woman's ability to let down. This has a great deal to do with the woman's ability to relax. There is an

Hispanic idea that milk will go sour if the mother is upset or angry. I do not know if the milk will go sour, but an upset woman may well have a harder time nursing. Sucking stimulation causes the cells around the alveoli and ducts in the breast to contract. The ejection reflex is called "let down." If a mother is tense or unhappy she may have trouble letting down, so even though the milk is there, the baby doesn't get it. Baby gets frustrated and sucks harder (creating sore nipples) and mom becomes more anxious. It is not the size of a woman's breasts but the state of her mind that is central to nursing. A relaxed mother who can truly focus on her baby is not likely to have this problem.

Enjoying nursing has a lot to do with letting go so you can let down. Don't worry too much about dishes in the sink or cobwebs in the corner. Get yourself a nice comfortable rocking chair, a cushion, a cup of tea and, while your baby's still too little to grab it out of your hand, a relaxing book. Use your nursing time for prayer and meditation. Enjoy. Let go and let it happen. What can be holier or more sacred than nurturing life and love?

Baptism

Baptism is the sacrament of rebirth. We are born into a family, but we are reborn into an entire community. Christians believe that through baptism we are purified, sanctified and welcomed into the body of Christ, who is the Church. Traditionally, baptism involves naming, the renunciation of sin and initiation into the Christian community. St. Gregory of Nazianzus says of baptism: "It is called *gift* because it is conferred on those who bring nothing of their own; *grace* since it is given even to the guilty; *baptism* because sin is buried in the water; *anointing* for it is priestly and royal as are those who are anointed; *enlightenment* because it radiates light; *clothing* since it veils our shame; *bath* because it washes; and *seal* as it is our guard and the sign of God's Lordship."[26]

At the time of baptism, we as parents acknowledge and commit to our role as our children's primary teachers in the faith. As parents, it is our responsibility to pass on our faith tradition to our children so that their lives may be enriched and strengthened as ours have been. Traditions have meanings, and when we hand on traditions we are passing on meanings to our children. As parents we are individuals, with our own beliefs and perceptions, our own doubts and questions. As Christians, we are also members of a faith community that professes certain beliefs and promotes certain teachings.

There will come a time for many of us when an aspect of our church's teaching may not reflect our own individual beliefs, or may simply raise doubts in our minds and misgivings in our hearts. Baptism is a good time to contemplate this issue and to ask ourselves, what will we do then? Do we jettison the problematic teaching from what we teach our children? Do we turn our children's instruction over to "more qualified" people? Do we put on a big smile and pretend we buy everything hook, line and sinker, without questions and without doubts? I do not know if there is a "right way" to handle this issue, but I think many parents will face the issue at one time or another. Let me share with you a little about how I handled it.

Baptism presented me with this problem. I love the teaching of the Mystical Body, the idea that somehow Christ connects us to one another, and somehow through one another we are connected to Christ. This is a mystery, yes, but a mystery that fits my experience and therefore makes sense to me. I could readily understand baptism as a sacrament in which the Church welcomes the infant into this sacramental experience of community.

What I had trouble with was the idea of original sin and the idea that this infant needed to be cleansed of sin. I looked into the innocent blue eyes of my children and I saw purity and holiness. I recalled the words of Jesus, "Whoever does not receive the kingdom of God as a little child will never enter it" (Mark 10:15), and I found myself asking: Why does this child need to be sanctified and purified? I knew of parents whose children were born too sick to live, desperate that their babies be baptized so that they would not be rejected by God. I know profoundly holy people among my Jewish friends, my Native American friends, my Buddhist friends who have never been baptized. I know in my heart that they are close to God.

My religious roots are in the Presbyterian Church and in Judaism. At 19 I chose Catholicism, but I am a very Presbyterian/Jewish/Catholic. My Protestant upbringing gave me a strong sense of individual conscience; my Jewish roots taught me to value, even revel, in controversy. I felt free to doubt the teachings on original sin. Catholicism has taught me not to be too sure of my own limited understanding, but to value authority and the teachings of others. I recall my husband saying to me as we debated this subject, "The teachings of the Church are the thinking of some of our greatest minds, pondering these mysteries over centuries. Why are you so quick to assume you know better?"

Although I felt free to question, I also felt I could not dismiss or take lightly the teachings of my chosen faith community. This meant that I had to struggle. I talked with people. I read various theologians on the subject. I prayed. And I learned. I learned that the belief that unbaptized infants would be condemned to hell was relatively recent, coming out of the 18th-century Jansenist movement, and not a tenent of my faith community. I learned that my faith community does not teach that humans are born corrupt, but rather that we are born vulnerable to ignorance, suffering and death.[27]

I began to understand that the idea of original sin was not about corruption so much as about vulnerability. Because we are social beings and grow up interacting with people who sin, we learn to sin. This did fit my experience. I could not see my child as evil and corrupt, but ignorant of sin, open and vulnerable to its influence? Yes. I could see that. I discovered that my understanding of my Church's teachings had been limited. It made sense to me that, given my children had been born into a world where sin existed, they would need to be strengthened by interaction with good and loving people. Through baptism, I was bringing my children into a safer place, a nurturing place, into the ark where they would receive the ongoing support they need to resist evil.

Most parents will not have the issues I had with baptism, but many will struggle somewhere along the way. Each of us will struggle with meanings professed by our faith community that, for whatever reason, are difficult for us. I believe that when we allow ourselves to struggle with these ideas, seeking knowledge and guidance in a spirit of openness and prayer, we are better able to pass on the traditions that will support our children throughout their lives. These struggles help us to grow up spiritually, so that we can be better fit to take on the truly humbling task of teaching our children about God.

Christian baptism may be administered by pouring, sprinkling or immersing in water. Water is a powerful symbol, for water is life-giving and cleansing. The breaking of one's waters signals the infant's descent through the birth canal. Water nurtures growth (as my poor garden reminds me every time I forget to water it). Water also symbolizes power and death. The flood destroyed all but a faithful handful of the Earth's inhabitants; the sea presented the obstacle, and the opportunity, to the Israelites' escape to freedom; the water destroyed their pursuers. In the early Church, the water ceremony was associated with the Easter Vigil, the sacrament of rebirth being associated with Christ's death and resurrection.

Many fonts are octagonal because the octagon symbolizes regeneration. Some early baptismal fonts were made in the shape of the womb. In the Greek Orthodox tradition, the baptismal font represents the divine womb in which the child is reborn as a child of God. In this tradition, a small amount of olive oil is added to the baptismal water.[28] The olive oil recalls the olive branch carried to Noah by the dove, telling Noah that the flood was over, that humankind was once again at peace with God.

For many traditions, baptism is given to infants; in other traditions, baptism is given when the child is older. For the first three centuries, adult baptism was the norm, although infant baptism was practiced from the second century on and possibly in apostolic times when whole households received baptism together.[29] Candidates for baptism, confirmation and Eucharist were called catechumens and entered into a preparation process. Lent was the church's preparation for baptism, which was celebrated once a year at the Easter Vigil. By the 5th century, this catechumanate process had practically disappeared in the Roman rite, and the sacraments of initiation had become three separate rituals. Infant baptism became the norm. In the 11th century, it became common to baptize children soon after birth due to the high infant mortality rate.

In recent years, some Christian traditions have returned to the catechumenate practices of the early church. In the Greek Orthodox tradition, a forty-day blessing period follows the child's birth and concludes with the child's baptism. The forty-day blessing, *sarantismo's*, reenacts the Presentation of Jesus in the temple forty days after his birth (Luke 2:22-35). In some households in Greece, visitors must wash their hands in holy water before holding the baby during this period.[30] The child is baptized with holy water and anointed with an oil called *miron*, receiving the gift of the Holy Spirit. The godparents, priest and a few selected children walk with the newly baptized infant around the font, symbolizing a dance of joy. The godparent presents the child to the parents, who kiss the hand of the godparent.

Baptism is associated with the naming of the child. When John baptized Jesus in the Jordan river, God named and claimed Jesus as the Son of God. To belong to a community is to be known by that community as someone. There can be no belonging without recognition. Naming recognizes the individual's unique self. When someone is baptized we name them, identify them and let the community know who they are.

In addition to the water ceremony, the child is often anointed with a perfumed, consecrated oil signifying the anointing by the Holy Spirit. In the Greek Orthodox tradition, the priest will make the sign of the cross with the oil on various places on the infant's body. The godparent may rub oil over the child's body, praying silently to God: "Oh God, let there be peace always between this child and you."[31] In the Roman liturgy, the anointing after baptism "announces a second anointing with sacred chrism to be conferred later by the bishop." Confirmation then completes the baptismal anointing.[32]

Traditionally, baptismal garments are white and signify "putting on Christ." In the early Church, the newly baptized wore a white garment for the fifty days of Easter.

Not only did they wear the garment, but they were expected to keep it clean. This must not have been an easy task. Imagine wearing a white outfit for fifty days while you eat and dig up weeds and clean house and put gas in the car. This provides a powerful symbol of the care it takes for us to live as children of light with clean hearts and minds in a world that is filled with the darkness and debris, the grime and grease of our human sinfulness.

In the Greek Orthodox tradition, the priest blesses the child's new clothing, which is then put on the child by the family or godparent. The priest then places a necklace with a cross around the child's neck. After the child is baptized, the child is placed in the arms of the godparent and wrapped in a white sheet, symbolic of the soul's purity. There is an old tradition of keeping this sheet to be used as a shroud when the person dies. In this way one is reminded that death, like baptism, is a rebirth.[33]

It is also traditional for the baptized person to be given a lighted candle. At birth we emerge from the darkness of the womb into the light of the world. Through baptism we are born into the light of God and bask in the light of God's people. There is an old tradition in which baptismal candidates turned to the west to renounce Satan and to the east, to the dawn, to accept Jesus. Traditionally, the baptismal candle was lighted from the Paschal candle at the Easter Vigil, to emphasize that we draw our light from the light of God. The baptismal candle can be purchased or easily made from a sheet of beeswax.

Baptismal Candles

Purchase sheets of beeswax and a length of wick from a craft store. Cut the wick about 1 $\frac{1}{2}$ inches longer than wax sheet. Place the wick approximately 1/4-inch away from the edge of the beeswax sheet. Bend edge of sheet over wick and press the edge to the sheet, molding them together. Continue rolling the sheet, pressing together as you go.

The candle can be decorated with baptismal symbols, cut from sheets of beeswax and pressed onto the candle or painted onto drip or molded candles with acrylic paints. Traditional symbols of baptism include a scallop shell with water dripping from it (calling to mind the baptism of Jesus in the Jordan river) and the phoenix which, legend tells us, makes a nest of sweet-smelling twigs and spices. The bird is consumed by fire when its nest is set on fire by the sun's heat (or, according to another version, by the fanning of the bird's wings). The bird is re-created out of its own ashes as we are reborn through the death and resurrection of Jesus.[34] Or you may wish to decorate the candle simply with a cross.

Keep the candle and use it on your child's feast days, birthdays and wedding day. One of our daughters keeps her baptismal candle on the chest of drawers in her room. She no longer lets us light it on birthdays and feast days for fear it will burn down, but it still has a place of honor on the table on such special days. When the candle is visible and used it becomes an ongoing reminder of the meaning of one's baptism.

Godparents, or sponsors, can play an important role and should be selected carefully. Christianity recognizes that, although the parents are the primary instructors of their children, they ought not to be expected to do the job alone. The godparent, or sponsor, takes on the role of helping in the child's spiritual upbringing. The godparent assists in the baptism and assists in the instruction of the baptized person. The godparent's role is of particular importance now when families are often bereft of the support of extended family members and close neighborhood relationships. Too often this role is a token role, and godparents do little to help the child grow up into a person of faith. What can a godparent do? What can parents request of the godparents they select?

Godparents often give religious gifts at the time of baptism, on feast days and birthdays. They join the family for special celebrations such as first communion, confirmation and the wedding. Sometimes it is the godparent who makes the child's Christmas stocking or sends the child an Advent calendar each year. When the child grows older, the godparents may send the child gifts that will encourage spiritual growth, such as a rosary or inspirational book. They may invite the child to spend a day with them, talking together and enjoying each other's company. Children appreciate having adults take an interest in their lives, their thoughts, their dreams and their needs.

In some traditions, the godparent's role is very significant. In the Greek Orthodox tradition, for example, the godparents often become members of the family and assume responsibility for the child's spiritual upbringing. They may provide the child with information regarding the significance of their name, give an icon of the child's patron saint, attend church with the child, and celebrate special days with the child, including the child's wedding.[35]

Godparents play an important role in Filipino tradition, where a child may have ten to fifteen godparents. It is an honor to be a godparent (and bad luck to say no). The godparents not only provide spiritual support as the child grows up but will take an active role in helping the young adult look for work. Godparents will be involved in the child's marriage and help him or her throughout life. It is customary for young people to visit all their godparents after Mass on Christmas.

It is often in adolescence that such a relationship nurtured throughout a child's life can blossom and bear fruit. At this age the child prepares to leave the nest and naturally seeks a trusted and understanding confidant other than (or in addition to) his or her parents. My husband and I are grateful that our adolescent daughters have strong spiritual adults they can turn to for advice, support and friendship.

Baptism is a time of rejoicing, not only for the family of the person baptized, but for the whole church, and therefore, it is a good time to give a party. There are many foods traditional for baptismal celebrations. Often baptismal foods are white or light-colored and sweet. White symbolizes the innocence of the newly baptized, and sweetness expresses the idea that being united to others in the church brings sweetness into one's life. In Lithuania it is customary for the godmother to bring a fruit bread or sweet cake and for the midwife to bring porridge.[36] Greeks often give bonbonieres, candied almonds that may be tied up in tulle with ribbons or placed in decorative containers that hold candles. There must be an odd number of candies, often seven, representing the seven sacraments.[37] Our family favors meringues. These meringues are light, sweet and pure, and can be made ahead.

Christening Meringues

Cover a cookie sheet with paper (unwaxed) and preheat oven to 250 degrees. Beat 2 egg whites (room temperature) until stiff. Gradually add while beating:

    6 tablespoons sugar
    1 teaspoon vanilla

Then fold in 2 tablespoons sugar. Drop spoonfuls onto cookie sheet so that they form peaks. Bake 50 minutes and remove gently with spatula.

In marriage, the love we share has its source in God's creative love. Birth calls us to affirm, proclaim and rejoice in the goodness and holiness of all creation through the care we give this new creation, our child. Spiritual traditions help us draw on the support of family, friends and our Christian community to strengthen and inspire us as we enter into our awesome new role of parenthood.

5

Rituals and Rhythms:
Everyday Holiness with Young Children

I recall a friend of mine telling me of his experience when he returned from the hospital with his firstborn child. As he crossed the threshold of his home, holding his precious bundle, he looked into his child's eyes and thought to himself, "He's never going away." It was a moment of wonder, exultation and alarm. From now on, this little human being would be at the center of his life, and his life would never be the same again.

Birth is a beautiful, miraculous event, but no more awesome than the immense reality that follows it; a human life has been placed into our hands and depends on us for everything. Some parents take to this new role like ducks to water. They seem to be at home with themselves and their children, taking on their new role with grace, ease and joy. For other parents, it is a difficult adjustment, a time of learning, insecurity and anxiety. For most of us, it is a bit of both. Parents may know and experience this new life as a blessing and yet at times experience the new tasks and responsibilities as a burden. Encouraged by our culture to focus on our own happiness, some of us are ill-prepared for the kinds of sacrifices parenting entails. How can our Christian tradition help us to treat our children as blessings rather than burdens, to live and give with joy rather than resentment, to act with faith rather than fear?

To be effective and joyful parents, we must learn to celebrate all of family life, both the extraordinary—special days like birthdays, feast days and holidays—and the ordinary, finding God in our mealtimes, bedtimes, playtimes, work times. We do this by creating ritual moments. Saying grace before a meal is a ritual moment. Blowing out the candles on the birthday cake is a ritual moment. Singing a lullaby to a child afraid of the dark is a ritual moment. Ritual moments communicate love and presence, meaning and hope. These rituals and traditions give our children something to count on, not once but again and again. When we learn to celebrate the ordinary, we begin to experience the extraordinary presence of God in our daily life. Living with this perspective helps us to experience our children as blessings rather than burdens.

It is good to begin creating and celebrating family rituals and traditions when your children are young. As we grow older, we often become more self-conscious and less open. Young children have an instinct for tradition. I remember the wise words of my mother-in-law not long after Teresa was born. "With children," she said, "once is a tradition." If you once buy an ice cream cone after grocery shopping, they are likely to expect an ice cream cone every time you go grocery shopping. If you get on the floor and play horsey when you get home from work on Monday, they are likely to be waiting at the door for the same game on Tuesday.

Young children are learning and absorbing information and behaviors at a rate no adult could attain. They are learning to talk, to walk and run and climb, to relate to others and to understand their environment. Small wonder that they need stability and consistency. Children who have an underlying structure they can count on are free to grow and develop. Children who grow up in insecure and inconsistent environments are likely to be fearful and inhibited. Familial traditions give children their daily dose of security.

For many of us, our religious or spiritual life has been a private thing. Yes, we attend church, but we would be uncomfortable if we were asked to be the celebrant or minister of a public service. When we become parents, we take on a role of spiritual leadership. My religious life is no longer a private affair. I now have a responsibility to help lead the spiritual life of my family. Some parents will feel uncomfortable, self-conscious and even a bit ignorant in this new role. We are no longer mere recipients of tradition; we have become builders of tradition.

Some of us come to our parental roles with a wealth of traditions gleaned from our own childhood. Others will create their familial traditions from scratch. This chapter provides a collection of ideas and experiences you may wish to pick and choose from. Or perhaps they will help ignite your own imagination, and you will create your own ritual moments. Here are some things to keep in mind as you get started.

Tradition-Building Tips

- **Keep it simple.** Simple is not stupid. Simple is not simplistic. Simple is core. Simple is essence. Simple is real and realistic. Most families today are overextended. If your home traditions are complicated and demanding, they will become just another chore rather than a source of meaning and hope.

- **Keep it joyful.** If you look at the traditions that continue to nurture people through the ages, you will find that most have an element of joy, even those that help us deal with death. Joy is exuberant. Joy is full of humor and hope. Joy is whole, enveloping our hearts, our minds and our bodies.

- **Let the actions speak.** In other words, don't preach. Ritual moments speak louder than words. Trust these moments. You won't need to tell your kids how meaningful something is if it truly is meaningful.

- **Become a learner.** Being a leader in your family or your community does not mean you become an expert. The best leaders continue to be learners. Sometimes as parents we think we have to know it all. We don't. To get comfortable with rituals and traditions, learn about them. Read books. Talk to other parents. Consult with religious leaders in your faith community. Be willing to learn from experience. Try on traditions. Experiment. You may need to adapt, alter or discard. Being a practicing Christian means just that. We need to practice.

- **Easy does it.** Begin slowly. Start out with little things. Traditions are like seeds sown into the ground of our lives. By their nature they grow and develop over time.

- **Let yourself be creative.** Feel free to use your imagination, to let your personality show. Sometimes we are afraid we will "do something wrong" or "say something stupid" so we hole up inside ourselves. This is hiding our light under a bushel.

- **Don't worry about being creative.** Sometimes we feel pressured to be new and relevant. Go ahead and lean on the past. That's what it's there for. God is always new and always relevant. We don't have to make God so.

Self-Care and Self-Sacrifice

Traditions offer us a way to give, and give from our depths. From the outset we must realize that through traditions of love and service and sacrifice, whether they be daily routines or annual celebrations, we pour ourselves out for our families. No one can sustain an ability to give unless there is a deep reservoir of grace and strength within. Any discussion of tradition-building must begin with a reminder of the need for a constant, fresh source of love and power.

Children are perceptive. They can tell if we are phony or real. I remember one of my mother's friends that my little brother called "the nasty sweet woman." To my knowledge, this woman never did anything mean to my brother, but her sweetness was unconvincing. She was a phony. We want our homes to be safe, loving places. As parents, most of us want to be nurturing, patient and kind. If we aren't feeling all that patient at work, most of us can fake it for a few hours; but you can't fake it with kids, and you can't fake it around the clock.

If we feel anger or resentment toward our children, they pick up on it. If we try to hide negative feelings behind a facade of sweetness, we are likely to come across as "nasty sweet." If our own spirituality is superficial, or our feelings about religion ambivalent, our children will pick up on that too. If we tell our children to live by one set of principles while we live by another, we will come across as phonies. Whatever traditions we choose to share with our children, they can only help us build a healthy, holy family life if they come out of something genuine within ourselves.

Today's parents often find issues of self-care and self-sacrifice confusing. If we do not nurture our own souls, we cannot hope to provide a spiritual environment for our children. This would be like a new mother trying to nurse her infant when she was fasting. And if we try to fake it, our children may not say so, but they will know. I do not believe there is any time in life when it is easier to neglect yourself than when the children are little.

My mother tells a story, funny in retrospect, of being housebound with the three older children (ages 5, 4 and 2 months). My mother didn't drive in those days and we lived in a big, old house in the country where there was no public transportation. My father was starting up a new business and worked long hours. One day, my mother called my father at work and asked him to stop by the library on the way home and pick up something for her to read. We had no television, and reading was my mother's way to relax and escape a bit from the demands of motherhood. My father (I think he was a little unclear on the concept) brought home several volumes of Kafka. Having nothing else to read at the time, she plunged into Kafka's dark, tormented world. It was a mistake. A young mother who has been home around the clock with three toddlers does not need a story about metamorphosing into a cockroach. She needs flowers, a back rub, a bubble bath, good music, someone to tell her she's gorgeous even in jeans and a T-shirt smeared with peanut butter.

One of the most difficult things for parents of young children is to have any balance in their life. When the child is quite young, you may wonder if you are ever going to sleep again. As they get a bit older and more mobile, you may begin to wonder if you will ever again have time to yourself. I do not find that parenting is any less total for parents who juggle jobs outside the home with parenting responsibilities. You don't stop being a parent when you're at the office. Your role as parent will tend to shape who you are and what you do outside the home, as well as in the home. Parenthood is a total experience. And the totality, no matter how much you love your kids, can get to you after awhile.

Christian families are called to live in community rather than in isolation and to learn to care for ourselves in a way that enables us to care for others. Self-care is a prerequisite for self-sacrifice, and self-sacrifice is an essential component of parenting. Christian traditions of parenting can help us to own our duties as parents, while helping us to care for ourselves in ways that enable us to be more caring of others.

What is self-care and what does it have to do with spirituality? How does self-care differ from selfishness? Self-care is about getting our own needs met, not through our children, but in our adult relationships and our spiritual life. The parents I work with often do not understand this. I think there is a relatively simple way to discern the difference between self-care and selfishness. Self-care increases my sense of inner peace and reorients me toward others. Selfishness intensifies my level of anxiety and dissatisfaction, causing me to turn in on myself, to become preoccupied with myself.

Parents of young children need to build in rituals of self-care. You will need to discover your own rituals, but let me share some that have worked for me. When my daughter Elizabeth was born, we were living with our in-laws, having just moved back to California. My mother-in-law had cancer and was dying at home. Naturally, the family was distraught. I was exhausted from caring for our 2-year-old and infant while helping to nurse my mother-in-law. At first, the four of us were living in a single room. There was no space, no privacy and precious little sleep. I realized that I was going to go crazy if I didn't do something, but what could I do? Parents are so often in this kind of position. You are called on to make healthy, thoughtful decisions that will affect your entire family when you are so tired you could cry. So what did I do?

Well, first of all, I had a good cry. It didn't change anything except my anxiety level, but that was a good beginning. Then I said to myself, Mary, what will help to keep you from going crazy? I recalled my mother's words, repeated to us so often in childhood. "What do you want for Christmas?" we'd ask. "A little peace and quiet," she'd say. That was what I needed. A little peace and quiet. Sounds simple, but believe me, for a parent of an infant and a 2-year-old, it isn't so simple. Hire a baby sitter, you say. Sure, that would be nice, but we couldn't afford a baby sitter. Ask a relative to help. Sure, I could ask someone to help out every now and then, but my relatives were caring for a dying mother and they had their own families and they worked. They didn't have a lot of time and energy to spare, and I needed a little peace and quiet not once a week but daily.

So I instituted quiet time. Some parents have nap time. I prefer quiet time for two reasons. First of all, children outgrow naps long before parents outgrow their need for nap time. Secondly, I like being honest with my kids, and the simple truth was that only one of my kids needed naps. My oldest daughter has an unusual metabolism and from birth needed less sleep than I do. Parents who gave me helpful advice about how to get this child to nap had simply no idea what I was dealing with. My mother-in-law, on the other hand, did know and confided to me that she regretted having prayed when my husband was little that he would have a child as active as himself. She explained that she hadn't thought back then about the mother who would be caring for this sleepless child. In any event, it wasn't little Teresa who needed some quiet time, but her mother.

Quiet time came after lunch. The children went into separate rooms. They didn't have to sleep and usually didn't, preferring to play peaceably. I spent that hour, not in catching up on chores, but in silence, prayer and reflection. That hour each day saved me. And I think it was good for the kids. Now that they are teenagers, they make their own quiet times for themselves. But I still have my quiet time. And when I shortchange myself my family can tell.

The temptation that I had, and that many parents have, is to fill up those precious bits of quiet time with work. Work is good; work is important; but when your children are little, work is endless. Giving up our luxuries, our pleasures, our time for our children is self-sacrifice. It is healthy and usually gives us a sense of well-being. Giving up whatever we most need to be healthy people is not self-sacrifice but self-destruction. It leads to resentment and either hostility, or hostility's ugly twin, phoniness.

Self-care is not self-indulgence. It is about taking a little time to see what you really need to be spiritually, emotionally and physically healthy, and then making sure you get those needs met. Perhaps you are someone who needs exercise and will need to work out or take walks. Perhaps you need to be around beauty. Make an outing to an art gallery or listen to music. Maybe you are a social person and really need some time with friends. Create traditions for yourself and your family that arise out of these needs. Meeting your spiritual and emotional needs is the first step in building a healthy family.

Christian traditions of parenting are rooted in the idea that children are a blessing and that parents have a duty to care for these blessings. I think it is important for us to recognize that in some ways our Judeo-Christian approach to the parent-child relationship is fundamentally different than that of American society. American society focuses on the principal of individual rights. In our society, a person has a right to have or not to have a child. Both parent and child have a right to the pursuit of life, liberty and happiness. The parent has a right to make decisions about his or her child's welfare. Parental rights and child rights can, and often do, conflict.

Judeo-Christian teachings, however, focus not on the rights of the parent but on the duties of the parent. This does not mean that parents do not have rights, but it means that the parent's duties to the child take precedence over parental rights. This may at first appear to be a subtle distinction, but it is a critical one. Judeo-Christian teachings can lead to a very different attitude toward parenthood than that found in our culture. In our tradition, God, not the parent, is the child's

Creator. The child belongs ultimately not to the parent, but to God. The child does not exist to fulfill the parent's needs or to make the parent happy.

Many parents in our culture are unclear on these basic principles. We often confuse self-care with selfishness, and self-sacrifice with victimization. Either way, our ability to be fully present to our dependent children is jeopardized. Child abuse is all too prevalent in our society. The topsy-turvy approach of the parent who focuses on his or her parental rights, whose own needs are unmet and feels the child exists to meet his or her needs instead of the reverse, is going to experience considerable conflict and stress in the parent role. The idea that the child is there to meet the parent's need is, in fact, the first indicator of potential abuse.

In our tradition, the needs of the child take precedence over the rights of the parent. The needs of the parent are to be met not by the child, but by the Christian community. From a Judeo-Christian perspective, parents are not expected to rear their children alone. One of the primary messages of baptism is that the community, not just the parents, has a responsibility to the child. The Christian community exists to help meet the parents' needs and to support the parents in their challenging role so that the parents can give more fully to their children. No Christian parents should feel they have to raise their child alone, or hesitate to call on their community to help meet their needs. All too often we as parents do not get the help we need because we do not ask for it. Jesus' words, "Ask and you shall receive," should be in the forefront of a parent's mind. I believe that a parent's ability to reach out to the Christian community for support is directly related to that parent's ability to love his or her children unconditionally.

In this book, I am discussing traditions for the home, but we can only minister to our families within our home if we are being ministered to by the community outside our home. We need to be responsible parents, seeing our children's care as primary, willing to make sacrifices on their behalf, but we need to draw upon our faith and our community for the strength to do this.

Mealtimes

Today is always the most important day in your child's life. It is not easy to celebrate daily life. Anything we do routinely we tend to take for granted. The importance of mealtimes and bedtimes and the other events that make up our days can so easily be lost. Daily life is not made up of Christmas presents and birthday cake. Daily life is made up of routines, mixed in with a dose of the unexpected and a seasoning of inconvenience. There is no need to make every day a big festival; that would only serve to make festivals routine. There is, however, value in learning to celebrate in little ways the important daily events that make up our lives. In her book, *Our Family Book of Days: A Record through the Years* (Denver, CO: Living the Good News, 1997), Kathleen Finley offers an excellent tool for building on this value in our families. She urges us to remember all the happenings in our family's life in a simple register.

When I asked parents what daily tradition was most important for their families, the answer I heard most often was "dinner." A Baptist minister told me that he had hard times when he was growing up, but his parents always managed to sit down to dinner with the kids. He believed that it was this daily meal that helped keep his family together and gave them strength. Now he and his wife both work. Daily dinner together seems to be impossible, but they make a point of having one family meal together each week.

I remember when I was young, my father was starting up a new business and worked long hours. Come six o'clock he was always there with the rest of the family at the dinner table. After dinner he often returned to work, but for that hour we were together, sharing our day's experiences with each other. As a child, I didn't realize what kind of effort must have gone into his commitment to the family dinner hour, any more than I appreciated the care my mother took in cooking and serving our meals. As a working parent, however, I understand that this daily ritual required a great effort on their part.

Jesus understood the importance of a meal when he broke bread with his disciples, saying, "Take, eat, this is my body which is given for you." He counseled us, his family, to eat together in memory of him. What makes mealtime so important? Eating is a physical act, but it is also a spiritual act. It nourishes both body and soul. In utero we are fed by our mother's body. As infants, we are nourished by milk from her breast. From the beginning, as we partake of food, we partake of relationship.

When people are deprived of food, they lose their ability to interact. Studies on human behavior during famine show that at the beginning of a famine, the search for food draws people together, heightening interaction and a sense of community. If, however, the famine continues, social interaction breaks down. People become aggressive and competitive. Relationships within the family erode until finally people sit silently at home, exhausted and isolated.[1]

This gives us some insight into the power of food and its relationship to community. A mild deprivation, such as that suggested by many Christian traditions, in the form of fast and abstinence days, can heighten our awareness of others and awaken us to a sense of community. Eating together gives us the opportunity to share and celebrate this community. When we break bread together, we nourish our bodies, our souls and our relationships. For Christians, then, meals offer physical nourishment, spiritual communion and the enrichment of family relationships.

What has happened to the family meal in America? In the United States, people suffer from poor nutrition in the midst of plenty, and the incidence of serious eating disorders, especially among young women, is on the rise. What's going on here, and what can parents do about it? We need, first of all, to value mealtime and to carve out times to eat together. Given the schedules many families have today, this is not always an easy task. Secondly, we need to find ways of making our family meals a time to enjoy one another and support one another. Human nature being what it is, this is not so easy either.

Meals are not just about food, fat content and calorie counting. Drinking an instant breakfast shake with the required daily dosage of vitamins simply does not give us what a sit-down meal with family and friends can give us. The family meals are so important in Filipino culture that everybody in the family eats three meals together each day if possible. These are usually two- or three-course meals that everyone shares. The emphasis is on sharing: sharing food, sharing thoughts, sharing stories that communicate family values, sharing an update of the day's experiences. The family makes decisions at meals and passes on family news.

Christian parents need to recognize that meals nurture body and soul; they have a priority that may require extraordinary efforts. Sometimes we need to set limits with our employers, choose at least one night a week to be free from outside activities, and turn off the TV. We need to adapt and be creative. Some families decide to get up twenty minutes early and eat breakfast together. I have great admiration for these families but I know this wouldn't work in my family. We're night people and even if I could manage to get everyone up and breakfast on the table, there is no chance anyone would have anything pleasant to say to one another. When we do eat breakfast together, we do better when ensconced in our books and newspapers.

Instead, we aim for dinners together. As a musician, my husband works odd, irregular hours. Often he doesn't get home until late. As a therapist and a chaplain, I work at least two evenings a week. Our children, involved in many activities, often have late rehearsals and meetings. I try to keep track of everyone's schedules and set the dinner hour to coincide with when we are all home. Sometimes we eat at 5:30 and sometimes not until 8:30. When dinner is going to be late, I try to put out veggies, fruit, bread and cheese to tide people over. On those nights when dinner together is impossible, we often gather together for a "bedtime snack" of hot cocoa and toast. We gather together in the kitchen or dining room and catch up on each other's news or joke around. For us, flexibility is essential.

Mealtime Blessings

Begin your family meals with a blessing. This is a time to remember God, the source of all that is good. It is a time to remember the needs of our own family and the needs of the world. Our family blessing is "Bless us, O Lord, and these thy gifts, which we are about to receive from thy bounty, through Christ our Lord, Amen." This is a Latin grace, said for centuries by Christians throughout the world: *"Benedic, Domine, nos et haec tua dona, quae de tua largetate sumus sumpturi, per Christum dominum nostrum. Amen."* Or try one of these other ancient mealtime blessings:

"Blessed be God, who in his mercy nourishes us from his bounteous gifts by his grace and compassion, O Christ, our God, bless the meat and drink of which we are about to partake, for you are holy forever. Amen."[2] (Greek Orthodox)

"Blessed are you, Lord God, King of the Universe, Who brings forth bread from the Earth." (Jewish)

Other suggestions:

- Invite different family members to begin the blessing.
- Allow a moment or two of silence for family members to add their own petitions, praying for friends or family members, as well as for those in the world who are suffering from famine or war.
- Keep prayers brief so the food doesn't get cold, or consider saying your blessings Jewish style at the end of the meal.
- Hold hands during the blessing.
- Try singing the blessing, especially if it is a special occasion.

If you have young children, your family meal may not feel or look much like communion. I recall my father-in-law describing their nightly dinners. "All five of the children were always given glasses of milk," he told me, "and every night somebody spilled their glass, all over the table, themselves, their sister, the dog." He shuddered visibly. "It was awful," he said. " I don't know why it never occurred to us not to give them glasses of milk at dinner." Little cartons of milk with straws would have helped. It may sound silly, but little things can turn family meals into a battleground instead of a time of communion.

When your kids are little, you sometimes wonder if they will ever be civilized. I was heartened, during these years, to read about the table manners of medieval nobility. They grabbed their food from a common bowl, gnawed on bones that they threw back into the bowl, spat on the table and wiped their noses on the tablecloth. In 1530, Erasmus suggested improvements in table manners in his popular treatise, *On Civility in Children*, which was reprinted thirty times in six years. In this work, Erasmus urged parents to teach their children to use only three fingers when dipping into the common bowl and to throw their chewed food behind their chair or under the table.[3] My children, in fact, were quite civilized...by medieval standards, that is.

It is because mealtime has power and because eating is as much about relationship as it is about food, that mealtime often becomes a power struggle and battleground. Children may complain about the food, refuse to eat the food, pick at their food and generally drive their parents crazy. Children don't have a lot of power, but they can control what they will swallow. Children will often choose mealtime as a time to assert their independence and personality.

Most families have rules, sometimes articulated, sometimes unspoken, about what is and is not acceptable at the table. When I work as a therapist with families, I often have them reenact a family meal. It gives me considerable insight into the family's dynamics: who gets heard, who is ignored, who is allowed to speak, who listens, who interrupts, who is interrupted, who starts fights, who makes the peace. Pay attention to these dynamics at your dinner table. The child who is always interrupted and never gets to finish a sentence is most likely to spill his or her milk.

Look for ways of giving each family member a voice, not just in family discussion, but in the meal itself. When I make up the grocery list, I ask the kids for their suggestions. I don't try to make each meal please everyone. In that way lies madness. I do try, however, to serve everyone's favorites frequently. At table, encourage each family member to talk about his or her activities and interests without ridicule or interruption. Make a point of complimenting family members for their accomplishments.

Do what works. Most of us have expectations of what a meal should be. Take an honest look at your expectations and be willing to discard those that don't fit your family's needs or are an unnecessary source of conflict. For example, when I was growing up we had a family rule that you had to finish everything on your plate. I remember my brother used to hold food in his mouth and refuse to swallow it. My parents would reason with him. "Just swallow it," they would say, "and then you won't taste it any more." Unfortunately, reason rarely works in this kind of situation. As we were beginning to raise our family, my mother told me she thought this rule had been a mistake. My husband and I decided not to insist that the kids finish their dinner. They can eat what they want and as much as they want, but they aren't allowed dessert unless they've finished their meal. The dessert rule is sacrosanct and nonnegotiable.

If the children absolutely hate something that's being served, they are allowed to substitute something else (provided that we agree it's equally nutritious and I don't have to fix it). I'm not a short-order cook and I won't fix more than one meal; but if one of the children prefers last night's dinner and heats it up in the microwave, that's all right with me. I used to think every meal had to have a cooked vegetable, starch and meat. We rarely eat cooked vegetables anymore. The children much prefer fresh vegetables and fruit, which are better for them anyway. I often fix these ahead and the kids will snack on them while dinner is cooking. In these rather simple ways we have avoided mealtime battles.

In some families, who cooks (and cleans up) is as important as what is cooked. I like to cook, but not everyone does. There is no rule that says mom has to do all the cooking. Consider taking turns cooking, or having different family members fix different parts of the meal. Children take pride in helping get dinner on, and should be thanked for their contributions. Our children have their own "specialties." Elizabeth is famous for her brownies and Teresa for her meringues.

Let your meals reflect your heritage as well as your family's personal tastes. Serve ethnic foods celebrating your family's roots and family recipes. Connect your meals with what is happening in the Church. Use a purple tablecloth and have an Advent wreath during Advent, a white tablecloth and lots of candles in the Easter season, a lily centerpiece on Marian feast days. Experiment, keep an open mind and you'll find what works for your family.

Little things can make meals more fun. Every now and then have a candlelight dinner, or have the children decorate the table for dinner. Creating a special centerpiece can be fun. Our children pick flowers from the garden for the dinner table. I have a friend whose child decorated their dinner table with his collection of miniature dinosaurs. One of my friends let her kids pick favorite dinner plates at a secondhand store. Her children liked having their personal plates. One of my daughters used to bring her stuffed animals to the dinner table to share our meal.

Some meals can be fun to eat, like fondue or tacos, where there is a variety of fillings for people to choose from. When they were little, my children liked "people salads" made from half a peach (for the body), a skirt of lettuce, arms and legs of celery or carrot sticks with raisin shoes, buttons and eyes, half a hard-boiled egg for the head (yolk down), with grated cheese hair. Teresa's favorite breakfast when she spends the night with Granny and Granddad is "bread soldiers." These are made from buttered toast cut into strips and dipped into a soft-boiled egg, cut in half and served in an egg cup. Kids eat better and family dinners are more enjoyable for everyone when food is fun.

Like most working moms, I've had to learn to cook meals that are not only nutritious and tasty but also quick to prepare. I rely a lot on broiled foods, stir frys and pasta dishes. The crock pot is a great invention for people who like foods that require slow cooking, but aren't home all afternoon to tend the stove. I make soups and pot roasts in the crock pot, throwing the ingredients into the pot before leaving for work in the morning. It is a great feeling to walk in the door after work and smell dinner already cooked and waiting.

Working Mom's Crock Roast

Before you leave for work in the morning, put half of the following vegetables in a crock pot:

    2 cups (approx.) baby carrots

    2 cans white potatoes, drained

    1 onion, sliced thin

Season with salt, pepper, oregano and basil. (May substitute a package of dry onion soup mix for onion and seasonings if desired.) Place a 3-4 pound beef brisket on top of vegetables. Add remaining vegetables. Then pour 1/2 cup beef broth and 1/2 cup red wine over everything. Cover and cook on low (10-12 hours) or high (5-6 hours), depending on your schedule. Serve with good bread.

Consider making a family or neighborhood cookbook. Invite family members (include aunts, uncles, grandparents, godparents) or neighbors to send you their favorite recipes. Print these up, put them into a decorative folder and send to neighbors and friends for Christmas. Somehow applesauce tastes better when you know it's Granny's recipe. And no one makes a better pizza than Uncle Bob. Using the recipes created by loved ones adds that ingredient so vital to any meal: love.

Consider serving meals with scriptural or religious significance. Begin the meal with a brief reading or prayer. For example, serve dishes with milk and honey. You might begin your meal with this prayer: "Dear God, you promised to bring your people out of slavery in Egypt into the promised land, a land flowing with milk and honey. We thank you for the sweet freedom in which we live and the good food you give us to eat. Amen." Serve milk shakes, milk toast or fresh fruit in cream. (Young children often love milk toast, which is subject to numerous variations, and wonderful fare for a sick child.) Make honey-orange butter with biscuits and honey-glazed chicken with a honey cake for dessert. (This honey cake also makes a great breakfast coffee cake.)

Milk Toast

Melt 2 tablespoons butter. Stir in 2 tablespoons flour and slowly add 1 cup milk, stirring constantly. Bring just to a boil, lower heat and cook until thickened. Dip toast in milk sauce and place on serving dish. Pour milk sauce over toast. Sprinkle with fresh chopped parsley, ham or hard-boiled egg. Or sprinkle with grated cheese and put in oven just long enough to melt the cheese.

Honey Glazed Chicken

Mix together:
   1/2 cup soy sauce
   1/2 cup honey
   2 teaspoons ginger
   1 large clove garlic, crushed
   1 tablespoon lime juice (optional)

Pour honey marinade over chicken pieces (approximately 6 pieces or one 3 pound fryer, cut up). Turn to coat chicken, cover and marinade 4-6 hours. Remove from marinade, cover with foil and bake at 350 degrees for 20 minutes. Uncover, brush with marinade and bake another 30 minutes.

Honey Cake

Mix together:

> 2/3 cup brown sugar
>
> 2 cups flour, pre-sifted
>
> 3/4 teaspoon baking powder
>
> 3/4 teaspoon baking soda
>
> 2 teaspoons cinnamon
>
> 1/2 teaspoon nutmeg

In another bowl, combine, mixing to blend well:

> 1/2 cup oil
>
> 1 egg, beaten
>
> 1/2 cup yogurt
>
> 1/3 cup corn syrup
>
> 1/2 cup raisins (optional)

Pour into greased pan. Then mix together and bring to a boil, stirring:

> 1/4 cup honey
>
> 1/4 cup milk
>
> 1/4 cup butter
>
> 1/2 cup sugar
>
> 2 tablespoons brown sugar

Remove from heat and add:

> 1/2 cup chopped pecans, almonds or walnuts

Spread over coffee cake before baking. Bake at 350 degrees 35 minutes or until done.

Honey Orange Butter

Cream 1 cup softened butter. Then add, blending:

> 1/3 cup honey
>
> 1 teaspoon grated orange peel

Another wonderful biblical story for children (because one of the main characters is a child), is the story of the feeding of the multitude with a boy's lunch of fish and bread. Read the story to your children and let them prepare an after-dinner skit for the adults while you prepare a meal of bread and fish. I was fond of pan-fried smelt when I was a child. Steamed fish is also wonderful, but even fish sticks will do. Use whatever your children are likely to enjoy.

Pan-Fried Smelt

Place 2 cups bread crumbs, 1 teaspoon seasoned salt and 1/4 teaspoon pepper in a plastic bag. Clean and dry smelt with paper towel and put in bag a few at a time. Shake to coat. Heat oil. Deep-fry fish until lightly browned and flaky; drain on paper towels.

Steamed Fish, Chinese Style

Rinse fish (which has been cleaned and scaled) in cold water and dry well with paper towels. Rub inside and out with salt. Fill pot with 2-3 inches of water. Place fish in heat-proof shallow dish on steamer rack in pot. Mix together:

    1 tablespoon sherry
    2 tablespoons soy sauce
    1 teaspoon rice vinegar
    1/4 teaspoon salt
    1/4 teaspoon sugar
    1 teaspoon shredded ginger root
    2 sliced green onions (saving
       some of green for garnish)
    1 garlic clove, minced

Place mixture on top of fish, cover and steam approximately 10 minutes (for a thin fish) or up to 25 minutes (for a thick, 2 pound fish). If water boils down, add more boiling water. Serve with rice and stir-fried vegetables.

One Native American belief saw the world as having six directions, each associated with the colors of corn: north (red), south (black), east (blue), west (yellow), up (white) and down (variegated).[4] When they shared corn with the early American settlers, they were sharing something sacred to them. Make a centerpiece of Indian corn. Serve cornbread, corn on the cob and sweet Indian pudding. Before your meal, pray: "We thank you God for this food, sacred to native peoples. We thank you for their generosity and for the generosity of all people who share with others. Teach us to be generous. Help us to make other people feel welcomed and at home. Amen."

Great-Grandma's Iowa Cornbread

Beat 3 eggs until thick and foamy.
Then add, beating until smooth:

    1 teaspoon salt

    2 cups buttermilk

    2 cups yellow cornmeal

Stir in:

    2 tablespoons melted butter

1 teaspoon baking soda dissolved
    in 1 tablespoon hot water

Pour into greased pan and sprinkle with a little cornmeal. The batter will be runny and the meal will sink to the bottom. Bake at 350 degrees for 30 minutes or until done.

Sweet Indian Corn Pudding

Combine in sauce pan, cooking and stirring until thick:

    3 cups milk

    1/3 cup molasses

    1/3 cup cornmeal

Combine in separate pan, stirring together:

    1 egg, beaten

    2 tablespoons butter, melted

    1/4 cup sugar

    1/4 teaspoon salt

    1/2 teaspoon ginger

    1/2 teaspoon cinnamon

Gradually add cornmeal mixture, stirring to blend. Pour into casserole dish and bake uncovered at 300 degrees for 1 1/2 hours.

Look for opportunities to let your meal reflect your values. I remember that during the Gulf War a small grocery store near where we lived, owned by Arab Americans, was vandalized and their plate glass window broken. The children and I walked to the grocery store, commiserated with the owners and bought Arab bread to use for our Sabbath meal that evening instead of the traditional hallah. It was a simple way to teach the children that we are people of peace, not people of hate.

Have a baking day and make bread, the "staff of life," or Scripture Cake. When you make bread together, wash the children's hands, and after washing, place your hands on each child's hands and say, "Bless the hands that prepare our food." Wash your hands and let the child say the blessing over your hands. When you eat the bread, pray: "Blessed be God, Ruler of the Universe, who brings forth bread from the earth." If you wish, say the blessing in Hebrew: *Baruch atah, Adonai Eloheinu, melech ha-olam, ha-motzi lechem min ha-aretz.*

This is my great-grandmother's recipe for Scripture Cake, which I've adapted to suit a modern kitchen. Mark the scripture passages ahead and read the passage just before you add the ingredient.

Scripture Cake

In a large bowl, cream together:
- 1 cup of Judges 5:25, last clause, curds (butter)
- 2 cups of Jeremiah 6:20, sweet cane (sugar)

Add, beating well:
- 6 Deuteronomy 22:6 (eggs)
- 1 cup of Judges 4:19, last clause (milk)
- 6 tablespoons of 1 Samuel 14:25 (honey)

In a separate bowl, mix together:
- 4 1/2 cups of 1 Kings 4:22 (flour)
- 2 teaspoons of Leviticus 23:17 leaven (baking powder)
- a pinch of Leviticus 2:13 (salt)

Season to taste with 2 Chronicles 9:9 (spice):
- 1 teaspoon cinnamon
- 1/2 teaspoon nutmeg
- 1/4 teaspoon cloves

Add dry mixture to wet, stirring. Then stir in:
- 2 cups of 1 Samuel 30:12 (raisins)
- 2 cups of Nahum 3:12 (figs, chopped)
- 2 cups of Numbers 17:8 (almonds, chopped)

Mix well. Pour into cake pans (greased and floured) and bake in a moderate oven (350 degrees) until done. Cake should spring back when touched in the center.

Another great way to enjoy scripture as a family is to have occasional theme meals. We have enjoyed more than one Noah's Ark dinner. Invite the children's stuffed animals. Make a centerpiece by using a wooden bowl or a toy boat for your ark. Let the children model animals out of colored clay to put in the bowl. Make a rainbow out of construction paper and suspend from the ceiling over the ark. Purchase a plastic white dove and glue an olive branch (cut from green paper) to its beak. Perch your dove on the edge of your ark. Put out shallow dishes of olive oil for dipping bread into and bowls full of different types of olives. Serve pizza with olives or *Aglio e Olio* (pasta in olive oil).

If you wish, put a little olive oil in a dish, scenting it with a few drops of perfume or lemon juice. Anoint your children by placing your thumb in the oil and making the sign of the cross on their foreheads. Pray: "May God bless you *(child's name)*. May God always be with you." After dinner you might want to read the story of Noah and the ark.

Noah's Ark Mealtime Blessing

Before you begin your meal, pray: "Dear God, you kept Noah, his family and the animals safe in the ark so that the world you created would not be destroyed. Keep us safe in your love. The dove brought Noah an olive branch as a sign that the flood was over and that you desired us to live in peace. Help us to be a sign of your peace in this world. With oil, Moses anointed the ark of the covenant. Help us to remember that you are with us just as you were with the Jewish people in the wilderness. With oil, King David was anointed; with oil the Good Samaritan anointed the wounds of the man who had been robbed and beaten. With oil we were anointed at baptism; with oil we are anointed in illness and at the hour of our death. May this oil help us to remember that you are with us always, in health and sickness, in life and death. Amen."

Aglio e Olio

Boil water for pasta. Follow package directions to cook 1 pound vermicelli or angel hair. Heat 1/3 cup olive oil in skillet. Sauté two crushed cloves of garlic. Drain pasta, mix with olive oil, season with salt and pepper. Add grated Parmesan cheese or chopped anchovies if desired. Or pass small bowls of cheese and anchovies at the table for people who want them. Serve with a green salad and good bread.

Bedtime Rituals

Most families with children probably have more rituals revolving around bedtime than around any other daily activity. Sometimes creative children who don't want to go to bed create these rituals as a delaying tactic. To understand the importance of bedtime rituals, it helps to understand why children don't want to go to bed. Even children who like going to bed have times when they will resist bedtime or will require elaborate rituals before surrendering to sleep. Bedtime removes the child from family activity. Some children just don't want to miss anything; others feel lonely. With bedtime comes darkness. The familiar and real give way to the unfamiliar and imagined. What's just a toy on the shelf in the daytime becomes a monster about to eat you up at night.

Bedtime is important because it helps us learn to deal with the unknown and the mysterious, with our fears and our dreams. Bedtime can also be a very intimate time between parent and child. Most of us learn to deal with fear in one of three ways. There is the whistling-in-the-dark approach, in which we simply pretend to be unafraid. Unfortunately, people who learn to ignore their fears are likely to put themselves at risk, for it is fear that warns us when we are in danger. Then there is the scaredy-cat approach, where we simply run away from anything scary. These timid souls are likely to live long, safe, unproductive and unrewarding lives, for it is difficult to accomplish anything or find fulfillment if we cannot face fear.

The third approach to fear is summed up by a dream my cousin had when he was little. He dreamed he was being chased by a huge, green, scaly, fire-breathing dragon with sharp teeth. He ran and ran and ran with the dragon right behind him. At last, he was so tired he just couldn't go on. So he turned around, faced the dragon and said, "Let's be friends!"

Acknowledging our fear, facing our fear and making friends with our fear is a very spiritual approach. God is mysterious, infinite and, scripture tells us, "greatly to be feared." The mystics who have experienced the most profound intimacy with God describe these experiences not only in terms of light and illumination, but in terms of darkness and unknowing. In teaching our children to face their fears of being alone in the dark, their fears of the unknown and the imagined, we are teaching them how to approach God. We do not want our children to pretend God isn't there, or to run away from God. We want our children to make friends with the mystery of God.

Bedtime, then, is a time for reconciliation, to make up, forgiving one another the hurts and disagreements of the day. Make it a tradition to apologize for any hurts you have caused. Parents sometimes shrink from admitting their mistakes, fearing such admissions undermine their authority. But our authority as parents resides in our duty toward our children, not in our perfection. We can hardly expect our children to admit their mistakes if they never see us do it. Bedtime is not a time to rehash an argument or prove a point. It's a time for loving, intimate conversations in which we can say that we agree to disagree, or that we're sorry, or simply, I love you.

It is good to begin winding down awhile before bedtime. Soft music, quiet conversation and bath time are all good ways to begin shifting from the activity and noise of the day to the stillness and rest of night. Most children love water and playing in the bath. Bath time can be a great way for children to unwind, and children often do need to unwind. They have ups and downs and tensions and worries too. You can make bath time special with bubbles, silly toys, even candlelight.

Bedtime is a time to reassure one another that our love for each other and God's love for us will be with us through the night. When children are very little we do this by singing lullabies and rocking a child to sleep. In our family we spent hours and hours rocking and singing. Even when the children got a bit older but were having a hard time, they might ask us to rock them and sing lullabies. There are so many beautiful lullabies. You don't need to be a great singer. Our children have been listening to our voices since the womb and will naturally find our voices comforting, whatever our vocal ability.

Take time to learn a few lullabies. They can calm both parent and child, and bring a sense of peace to the entire household. Often I have seen an older child or one of the adults hovering at the bedroom door, listening as the infant is sung to sleep. A song doesn't have to be a traditional lullaby to become a child's bedtime favorite. For some time Elly's favorite "lullaby" was "Clementine." As children get older, reassurance is given in other ways: a hug, a kiss, a back rub, a story (read or made up) or quiet conversation. But music is still a great source of comfort. Record your favorite lullabies on a tape. Even my teenagers have been known to listen to these lullaby tapes while drifting off to sleep.

All Night, All Day

traditional spiritual

Baloo Balelee

traditional Scottish

Ba- loo ba- le- lee. Ba-

loo ba- le- lee. Ba- loo ba-

le- lee Ba- loo ben noo.
1. Gae a-
2. Doon
3. Tae

wa peerie fairies. Gae a- wa peerie
come bonnie angels, tae warm peerie
sheen oor the cradle, tae warm peerie

faeries. Gae a- wa peerie faeries. Gae a-
bairnie. Doon come bonnie angels, tae
bairnie Tae sheen oor the cradle, tae

wa ben noo.
oor ben noo.
warm ben noo.

Translation: Go away little fairies from the inner room.
Come lovely angels to warm the little child.
To shine over the cradle, to warm the inner room.

All Through the Night

traditional Welsh

1. Sleep my child and peace attend thee, All through the night.
   Guar- dian an- gels God will send thee, All through the night.
2. An- gels watching e– ver round thee, All through the night.
   In thy slumber close surround thee, All through the night.

Soft the drow-sy hours are creep-ing, hill and vale in slum-ber sleeping.
O'er thy spir- it gent- ly steal-ing, vi- sions of de- light re- vealing

I my lov-ing vi- gil keeping. All through the night.
Breathes a pure and ho- ly feeling. All through the night.

Night Prayer

Bedtime rituals reassure us of the abiding presence of love in the face of the dark, the unknown and the mysterious. The most ancient Christian bedtime ritual is Night Prayer, which dates back to the early Christian communities. Night Prayer was a brief prayer said at bedtime. It was the last act of the day, in which the Christian entrusted his or her life to God. It was believed that God continued to guide the soul even in sleep.[5] As the psalmist writes, "I bless the Lord who gives me counsel; in the night also my heart instructs me" (Psalm 16:7).

Scripture and Christian tradition are filled with examples of people being guided by God through nighttime dreams and visions. The angel of God spoke to Jacob in a dream (Genesis 31:11). Joseph had many dreams showing him God's will and he later became an interpreter of the pharaoh's dreams (Genesis 37–41). Daniel also interpreted dreams (Daniel 7:1), and an angel appeared to Joseph in a dream (Matthew 1:20) telling him not to be afraid of taking Mary as his wife. He was again warned in a dream to take his family to safety (Matthew 2:13).

From a spiritual perspective, we believe that God comes to us in our dreams. From a psychological point of view, it is often at night that the unconscious mind reveals to us inner truths our conscious minds may be unwilling or unable to grasp. The Christian tradition of Night Prayer teaches us how to approach this fertile darkness.

Night Prayer is filled with words of hope and prayers for peace and reconciliation. It is a time to make peace with our loved ones, with ourselves and with God, forgiving one another and receiving forgiveness. Night Prayer not only prepares the Christian for the night, but for death, ending with the simple blessing: "The Lord grant us a quiet night and a perfect end."[6] We do not like to think about death when we think about children. We tend to avoid the subject in their presence; but young children do grapple with the idea of death and have very real and profound experiences in dealing with loss and grief. Like adults, their fears and worries and sorrows often surface in the lonely stillness of night. Children are not, after all, afraid that the monster of their nightmares is going to tickle them. No, they fear being hurt or killed. We do children no favor to pretend they are too young and innocent to be touched by such fears. There is great wisdom in the Night Prayer blessing, which accepts darkness and death as a natural part of life.

Bedtime is a time to place ourselves wholly in God's hands. It is a time of prayer, a time to ask the darkness to be our friend. There are many beautiful books of prayers, traditional prayers, contemporary prayers, prayers for children. The psalms are among the loveliest of prayers. Take some time at a book store or local library, or ask other parents, and collect bedtime prayers your family especially likes. We collected various prayers and then made our own book of bedtime prayers. We left blank pages for prayers we would find in the future, encouraged family members to write a few prayers of their own and illustrated it with cut-out pictures and the children's drawings. Teresa made a "stained glass" candle holder by gluing colored tissue paper onto a jar and we placed a votive candle inside. The children took turns picking a favorite prayer, and lighting the candle. We would have a moment of silence, the selected prayer and a time for the children to pray for their special concerns. We ended with a song, such as "An Evening Prayer," on the next page.

Sometimes parents bless their children after tucking them in. Other parents like to say the same prayer every night. We used to say the Our Father and the *Shema:* "Hear, O Israel: The Lord is our God, the Lord is One" (Deuteronomy 6:4). Some families say a decade of the rosary or the Hail Mary. I wanted the children to grow up with the traditional prayers of the Church in their hearts and minds, but I also wanted them to be able to talk to God in their own words, so we combined traditional and personal prayers.

Children often have other rituals: a bedtime snack, certain blankets and stuffed animals that have to be in just the right position, the light on or off, the door open three inches, not four. Our children always had tapes to listen to after they'd been tucked in, usually lullabies or classical music such as Mozart, Chopin, Bach.

These are all ways of helping the child feel more secure as he or she faces the mystery of night.

An Evening Prayer

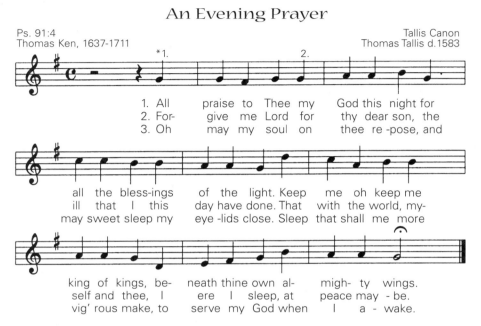

Ps. 91:4
Thomas Ken, 1637-1711

Tallis Canon
Thomas Tallis d.1583

1. All praise to Thee my God this night for
2. For- give me Lord for thy dear son, the
3. Oh may my soul on thee re -pose, and

all the bless-ings of the light. Keep me oh keep me
ill that I this day have done. That with the world, my-
may sweet sleep my eye -lids close. Sleep that shall me more

king of kings, be- neath thine own al- migh- ty wings.
self and thee, I ere I sleep, at peace may - be.
vig' rous make, to serve my God when I a - wake.

*Can be sung as a round, with the second voice beginning when the first voice arrives at number 2.

Another important bedtime ritual is the bedtime story. Many parents read to their children. Sometimes the children would gather in our bed for story time, or on the couch. There are so many wonderful stories to read children. You might read a story a night, or choose a chapter book and read a chapter a night. Biblical stories and folk tales lend themselves to dramatic retellings.

Some parents who travel on business use story time as a way of maintaining contact with their children. They call at bedtime and "conference call" the bedtime story. When we are gone on trips we tell stories on postcards (usually "to be continued" cliff-hangers), which derive their inspiration from the card's picture. Our children like made-up stories. The children get to pick various items that must be included in the story (such as a porcupine, a dish of green Jell-O and an astronaut named Fred). Their memories are excellent and they will correct the sleepy parent who leaves out a required item.

Sometimes bedtime stories become multi-generational traditions. My father-in-law's stories were so famous with his children and later with his grandchildren that we had to have tapes made of them. Bedtime stories feed the child's active imagination with rich symbols, images, characters and events. Some religious writing (and illustrating) aimed at children is dull, humorless and a bit preachy. A story with a proper moral that lacks beauty or humor will do little to nourish your child's soul.

The subject of dreams and the spiritual life of children is so rich and important it really could be a book in itself. In many cultures parents teach their children how to listen to their dreams and how to integrate their dream life into their daily life. We tend not to pay much attention to dreams and this is a mistake. Our dream world is a fertile world. Parents can encourage their children to tap into this rich world of dream by praying with the children at night that God will guide their dreaming, talking with them about their dreams the next morning and encouraging older children to keep a dream journal. Share stories with your children about saints, prophets and holy people who have been guided by dreams. Share some of your own important dreams. Not every dream is of significance, but some are. It is good for a child to grow up open to this inner world, able and willing to draw upon it for insight and strength.

Family Prayer

We have already discussed family prayer at mealtime and bedtime. Many families set aside other times to pray together. If you wish to have a family prayer time, setting a regular time (after family dinner on Friday, for example) and having a simple structure helps. Some families say a mystery of the rosary together. Others read a passage of scripture. Sometimes different family members take turns reading verses, reflecting silently or sharing thoughts the scripture inspires. Others families hold hands and offer up petitions or words of praise in their own words. Some families like to sing hymns together, others may say Evensong. Different family members can take turns preparing for and leading the family prayer.

In many Catholic families, it is traditional to pray together at the ringing of the Angelus. By the 14th century, it had become customary to ring church bells at 6 a.m., noon and 6 p.m. to call people to honor Mary and remember the Incarnation. The Angelus (from the Latin for angel) may be said by one person, but is often said by the family together.

Angelus

Leader:	The Angel of the Lord declared unto Mary.
All:	And she conceived of the Holy Spirit. Hail Mary, full of grace, the Lord is with thee. Blessed art thou among women and blessed is the fruit of thy womb, Jesus.
Leader:	Behold the handmaid of the Lord.
All:	Be it done onto me according to your word. Hail Mary. . .
Leader:	And the Word was made flesh:
All:	And dwelt among us. Hail Mary. . .
Leader:	Pray for us, O holy Mother of God.
All:	That we may be made worthy of the promises of Christ.
Leader:	Let us pray: Pour forth, we beseech you, O Lord, your grace into our hearts; that as we have known the incarnation of Christ, your Son by the message of an angel, so by his passion and cross we may be brought to the glory of his resurrection. Through the same Christ, our Lord.
All:	Amen.[7]

The saying of the Angelus is an important tradition for Filipino families. Children know they must be home to say the rosary with their family by six o'clock when the bells ring. Prayers are followed by dinner. Vietnamese Catholics traditionally pray the rosary and litany of the saints together before bedtimes.

Many Catholic families keep a font of holy water by the front door. Family members bless themselves with the water upon entering and leaving the house. One man told me that when his mother reminded them to bless themselves with holy water before leaving the house she would always say, "Remember who you are." Such prayer rituals do, indeed, remind us of who we are, encouraging us to take the Christian values of our family life with us into the world of school and work.

Another helpful prayer tradition for families is the "prayer tree." To create a prayer tree, contact extended family members and friends who are willing to pray for each other. Each person on the list agrees to call another person on the list. If anyone on the prayer tree is ill or in need, you call your contact person on the list and he contacts his person, who contacts his person. Soon everyone on the list is praying. Prayer trees are most often used when someone is ill or in crisis, but there is no reason why one can't use the prayer tree to give thanks for a new baby or a new job or success on a difficult school test.

Home altars are traditional in many cultures. Vietnamese Americans often have ancestral altars where flowers, fruit and incense are offered on special days. This is a way of honoring the memories of those who have died, keeping a strong connection between the living and the dead. In other cultures, home altars are set up for special feast days. Mexican Americans may honor Our Lady of Guadalupe on December 12 by creating a home altar. This may be done by covering the walls of the room with white sheets to which colorful flowers are pinned in rows from floor to ceiling. An altar is set up and decorated with pictures or statues of Our Lady. A meal is served and family and friends gather for a day of feasting, prayer, song and dance. This lovely song, "Buenos días, Paloma Blanca," is traditionally sung to welcome Mary on the morning of her feast.

Buenos Días, Paloma Blanca
(Good Morning, White Dove)

del Crea- dor Ya a mi cor- a-

zon en- can-ta. Gra-cias te doy con a-

mor. Bue-nos días, pa- lo- ma blan-ca.

Verse 2: Eres madre del Creador y a mi corazón encantas. Gracia te doy con amor
Buenos días, Paloma Blanca

Verse 3: Niña Linda, Niña Santa, tu dulce nombre alabar porque sois tan sacrosanta
Hoy te vengo a saludar.

Verse 4: Reluciento como el alma pura, sencilla, y sin mancha qué gusto recibe mi
alma, Buenos días, Paloma Blanca

Translation

Verse 1: Good morning, white dove, today I come to greet you, hailing your beauty in
your celestial reign.

Verse 2: You are the Mother of the Creator, and you enchant my heart. I give you
thanks with love: Good morning, white dove.

Verse 3: Lovely Maid, holy Maid, your sweet name be praised. Because you are so
sacrosanct today I come to greet you.

Verse 4: Luminous as the soul, pure, simple and without stain, what pleasure my soul
receives. Good morning, white dove.

Italian Americans traditionally set up a home altar on St. Joseph's Day, March 19.
These altars are often built as an act of gratitude for answered prayers. The altar
and walls of the room may be decorated with lace or religious tapestries and a
large table is loaded down with food, including fruits, breads, fish, cookies, cakes
stuffed with figs and a pasta made with spaghetti, bread crumbs, celery and grated
cheese. An abundance of food is made so that there will be plenty of leftovers to
distribute among the needy of the neighborhood. A picture of the Holy Family
may be placed on the table and places saved for Jesus, Mary, Joseph and various
saints (as many saints as there are children present). The children play the part of

the Holy Family and saints and go from house to house in the neighborhood; each household turns them away until they are welcomed into the chosen house, invited to sit at the table and are waited on.[8]

Some families set up a prayer corner, a quiet place conducive to prayer, which may include religious pictures or statues, a Bible, rosary, candles and other aids to prayer. You may wish to personalize your prayer corner by encouraging your children to place in it whatever speaks to them of God (such as a perfect seashell found on the beach, a picture of the family pet or a picture they have made).

Family Meetings

Families have numerous decisions to make together. Many families find it helpful to set aside a regular time to discuss family "business." Almost anything can be discussed at these meetings, from planning the family vacation to discussing family chores. At the family meeting, individual family members, both parents and children, can raise issues about family rules (bedtime, television, etc.), to hash out differences and arrive at solutions. Family meetings also offer an opportunity to congratulate a family member on an accomplishment or to say thank you for helping out. For family meetings to work well, there need to be a few simple ground rules so that each person feels he or she will be heard and respected.

Tips for Family Meetings

- Everyone gets a turn to talk.
- No interrupting.
- No name calling.
- Set your meeting length to be short and sweet.
- Begin and end your meetings on a positive note.
- Compliment your children for good suggestions and for taking risks in expressing their feelings.
- Reward yourselves for especially good meetings with a family game or a snack.

There is a wonderful Native American tradition in which a sacred stick is passed during a meeting. When you are holding the stick, you must speak from the heart and no one should interrupt you. After you have spoken, you pass the stick to the next person. I have used this with families suffering from communication problems and found it not only helps the children to be respectful of each other, but also the adults. Family meetings can help families develop good communication. (An excellent book to read on family communication is Virginia Satir's *Peoplemaking* [Palo Alto, CA: Science & Behavior Books, 1972].)

Helping Others

There is no better way to teach children to be generous and helpful than by modeling this behavior in our own lives. I recall two scenes from my childhood that had a great impact on me. One weekend we went camping, and the family in the campsite next to us—a husband, wife and four children—were homeless and living out of their station wagon. My parents invited them to come home with us. They set up beds for them in the family room and my mother cooked a big dinner. They stayed with us for several days and then went on their way. My parents didn't need to tell me why this family had been invited to stay with us; I understood. I knew that my parents considered the poor and hungry to be Christ present among us.

I remember another time when a strange, disheveled man came to the door. He smelled bad and spoke in an odd, somewhat incoherent way. We lived in a big old house out in the country and my mother and I were home alone, but my mother invited the strange man in and fed him a bowl of soup. It was not convenient to house and feed a family of six without a moment's notice and there are many who would, understandably, have hesitated to let a strange old man into their home. At these moments I do not think my parents were trying to teach me about being a Christian. They were simply being Christian; but the lesson came through loud and clear. To be a Christian, I learned, is to go out of your way to care for the needy of this world.

Many parents are concerned about how to give their children good self-esteem. One way is to bless them and affirm them; another is to teach them to help others. It is in helping others that we discover what we have to give. Any person of any age has much to give, but you cannot discover how much you have to offer until you make your offering. There are many helping traditions in our Judeo-Christian heritage: traditions of hospitality and traditions of tzedakah, or charity. These traditions date back to Abraham and Sarah who, in welcoming the stranger, entertained angels (Genesis 18).

In Jewish tradition it is a *mitzvah* (commandment) to have guests at one's table. We must provide for the stranger and for those who do not have families of their own, remembering what it was like to be strangers in the land of Egypt. In the Talmud *(Shabbat 127a)*, Rabbi Judah teaches that "welcoming guests is of greater merit even than welcoming the presence of God."[9] One New Testament writer refers to Abraham's angelic guests when he urges the early Christian communities: "Do not neglect to show hospitality to strangers, for by doing that some have entertained angels without knowing it" (Hebrews 13:2). In the Greek Orthodox tradition, the importance of hospitality, *philoxenia*, dates back to ancient times. One was expected to receive a traveler as a member of one's own family, and even enemies were entitled to hospitality.[10] St. Benedict taught, "Let all guests that come be received as Christ Himself, for He will say, 'I was a stranger and you took Me in.' "[11] A Polish proverb says that "a guest in the home is God in the home." This is truly the Christian approach to hospitality. The stranger in our midst, the guest, is God, once again coming to us in human form.

Another way of extending our hospitality is by giving food to friends, neighbors and those in need. Christian hospitality is taking a casserole to someone whose family member is ill or injured, or to a family suffering the loss of a loved one; it is welcoming neighbors with cookies and coffee cakes and setting a place for the stranger at your table. My grandmother used to tell me, "Often comes Christ in the stranger's guise."

The Hebrew word, *tzedakah*, comes from *tzedak*, meaning "justice." Deuteronomy 16:20 teaches "Tzedak, tzedak tirdof—justice, and only justice you shall pursue." The Judeo-Christian concept of charity comes from this justice. We are merely stewards of the Earth's riches, for creation belongs not to us, but to the Creator. The needy person is God's child and, as such, has a right to share in the goodness of creation. To help the helpless is never condescension, but justice.

In the Jewish tradition, there is tzedakah of the body and tzedakah of the soul. We are to reach out to those who are in physical need, but also to those in spiritual need.[12] To feed the hungry or give clothing to the poor is tzedakah of the body. Visiting the lonely or singing to lift the spirits of those who are weary with life or weighed down with sorrow is an example of tzedakah of the soul. It is an ancient tradition to keep a tzedakah box in one's home and to put money into it before praying. Even the poor kept a tzedakah box, enriching their souls through their generosity.[13] The money from the box is given to the needy. In many Christian homes it is traditional to keep a box for money to be collected for the poor during Lent. People deny themselves certain luxuries during Lent and put the money in the box to be given to those in need.

Many families choose to get involved in community projects and organizations that work to meet the needs of others. Volunteering at a soup kitchen, helping to repair and rebuild homes for the poor with Habitat for Humanity, participating in food drives and fund-raisers for shelters, medical and counseling services, sponsoring an orphan, singing for people in hospitals or nursing homes, turning vacant lots into gardens—these are but a few of the many ways for you and your family to get involved in making the world a more just and holy place. So many people grow up these days with a feeling of helplessness. Knowing your life can make a direct, immediate difference in the life of another human being can give you a much needed sense of hope and purpose.

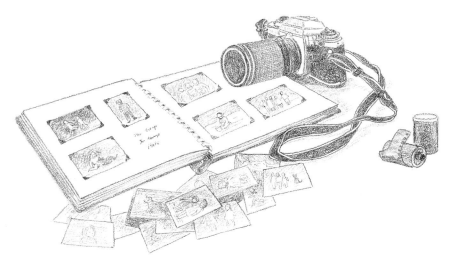

6

Marking the Years: Highlights and Holy Days in a Family's Life

We have been exploring the rituals of daily life: mealtime, bedtime and time for prayer and service. We also celebrate special days of honor in our family's life. Birthdays, name days and feast days acknowledge the growth and proclaim the personhood of individual family members. Family parties following baptism, first communion and confirmation celebrate spiritual milestones, helping us to see and give thanks for our spiritual growth.

Jesus periodically withdrew from the demands of teaching, preaching and healing to spend time with his heavenly Father and with his closest friends. Our families also need to slow down every now and then and let our batteries recharge. Vacations and pilgrimages are important times for family togetherness, relaxation and renewal, as are the weekly holy days of family life that we call Sabbath and Sunday.

When Jesus needed to "recharge," he often went into the hills or into a garden. For centuries people have been seeking their Creator in gardens. Planting and tending a garden is another way for our families to experience God with us as we celebrate the seasons and the ongoing cycle of birth, growth, death and rebirth.

These channels of the Spirit that we recognize in extraordinary ways shape our lives deep within. It is right and good that we honor the Spirit's work with thoughtful, joyful and creative celebrations.

Birthdays and Namedays

Birthdays and feast days are the days on which we celebrate the life, uniqueness and personhood of each member of the family. They are days when we celebrate the blessing of birth.

Feast Days, or Name Days, are an old Catholic and Orthodox custom, in which the family and friends celebrate on the feast of a person's "baptismal saint," that is the saint after whom one has been named. This saint is considered a personal patron. Traditionally, children are taught about their saint, attend church on their patron saint's feast day and are congratulated at a family celebration following. Often children are given a medal of their patron saint to wear, or may have a statue or picture of their saint in their bedrooms.

The tradition began in the first century, when Christians would gather in the catacombs to pray together on the anniversary of a martyr's death.[1] Christians began to name their children after these saints. You can still see frescoes of these gatherings in the catacombs. The tradition calls for attending Mass early in the morning of your nameday and sitting down to a festive breakfast afterward. The child celebrating his or her feast day is excused from regular chores and receives presents.[2] In Europe, the nameday is the primary celebration, and the birthday may receive little attention. Namedays are a wonderful way to encourage your children to emulate and become familiar with model Christians. If your child does not have a saint's name, let him or her pick one. A good dictionary of saints can tell you the date of your child's feast day or help you choose a saint for your child to emulate.

There are many traditional foods for nameday celebrations. *Kugelhopf* is a traditional European nameday cake. In the Russian Orthodox tradition, a special sweet pretzel called *krendlis* is served.[3] Mexican Americans may serve eggs. The Mayans fed babies eggs to give them understanding. Later, eggs came to symbolize life and prosperity. In the Christian tradition, eggs became a symbol of the resurrection. The chick bursting out of its shell spoke of Christ rising from the tomb. Tamales and pork mole (made with a chili, garlic, chocolate and peanut butter sauce) are also traditional in Mexican American homes for namedays and other festive occasions.

126

In Yugoslavia, it was traditional to serve spit-roasted lamb at nameday celebrations.[4] In Greece, namedays are often celebrated with an open house. No invitation is needed. One may go from open house to open house of each friend named after the saint whose feast day it is. In the United States, nameday parties are often given. Greek Orthodox children may attend church with their parents and/or godparent. A flower or bouquet may be placed by the saint's icon in the home or church.[5] Evelyn Vitz's *A Continual Feast* is an excellent resource if you wish to celebrate namedays. *Catholic Household Blessings and Prayers* has a number of blessings for namedays and birthdays.

The first birthday party in recorded history was given by an Egyptian pharaoh. Although in many parts of the world it is more popular to celebrate namedays, birthdays get the most attention in the United States. Birthday celebrations include inviting the child's friends for a party, but they are also important times for the family to celebrate. A birthday is a good time for parents to give their child a blessing. The parents, grandparents and godparent may take turns placing their hands on the child's head and praying for the child. You may pray in silence, in your own words or use a traditional prayer. Some families take time at the birthday celebration to go around the table, allowing each person to say what they love about the birthday boy or girl. If you want to do this, let family members know ahead so that they can be prepared. If a family member is uncomfortable saying this out loud, write down the blessings and affirmations. Adapt your rituals to fit the comfort level of the participants. One tradition invites each family member (be sure to include grandparents, aunts, uncles and siblings) to write down a few words that express what he or she admires about the birthday child. These can be gathered together in a special box or little book and saved for the child to read and reread later.

Let your child participate in planning the festivities, picking the color for tablecloth, napkins and balloons, picking the games to play, songs to sing, favors to give and food to eat. Play your child's favorite music. Put the child's baptismal candle in a place of honor on the table and decorate the base with flowers. If you have a favorite photo or painting of your child, place a flower beside it. Make a visit to church and light a candle in thanksgiving for your child.

If you planted a tree when the child was born, decorate the tree on his or her birthday. You might even give the tree a gift of a birdhouse. We like to brush melted lard on pine cones, sprinkle them with seeds and tie them to the tree for the birds. Let the kids decorate the house. Hang a birthday banner or flag or tie a bouquet of balloons to the front porch. Give the birthday child breakfast in bed. Place a bouquet of flowers in his or her room. A tradition in our neighborhood that I especially love is the tradition of decorating the front yard with wooden figures (penguins or flamingoes or rabbits, for example). The number of figures corresponds to the number of years.

Among Filipino Americans, birthdays are a big family event and everyone gathers in the house for a party. It is traditional to serve a noodle dish and lots of ice cream. The noodles, because they are long, symbolize long life and prosperity. If one is unable to have a birthday party, a huge pot of noodles is cooked, put in carry-out boxes and sent to family members. Here is a recipe for Birthday Noodles that I have adapted from a recipe sent to me by Father Garcia, a priest I met through the Office of Ethnic Ministries of the Archdiocese of Chicago.

Pancit Bijon Guisado

In 1/4 cup oil, sauté 2 cloves of minced garlic. Add:

- 1 onion, minced
- 1 cup cooked, sliced pork
- 1 small cabbage, shredded
- 2 tablespoons soy sauce

Cook over medium heat, stirring, 2–3 minutes. Then add:

- 1 1/2 cups chicken or vegetable broth
- 1 bunch kintsay or Chinese leeks, sliced diagonally

Simmer until vegetables are cooked (but not limp). Soak and drain 1 bundle bijon (rice sticks) and add to vegetable mixture, stirring. Season with 1 teaspoon salt (or to taste) and 1 teaspoon Aji-no-moto. Put noodles and vegetables into serving dish and top with:

- 2 pieces chorizo canton (Chinese sausage), sliced and fried
- 1 spring onion, chopped

In the United States, birthday cake is traditional, decorated with the child's name and candles numbering the child's age. The lights are turned off, the candles lit and mom or dad carries in the cake, placing it in front of the birthday boy or girl. The child makes a wish, blows out the candles and, if old enough, cuts the first piece.

An Hispanic tradition that has become popular in the United States, both for Christmas and birthdays, is the *piñata*. I recall the year my mother and I made a piñata for my birthday. We cut out the sides of a box and covered it with tissue paper, fashioning a head from a smaller box, and eyes, ears, tail and legs from construction paper. He was a wonderful white donkey that we spent hours making and then gleefully bashed to bits, letting loose a shower of candies and pennies. If you make a piñata with your child's help, make sure your child is really willing to have his or her creation destroyed. You may need to have a backup for bashing as not all children enjoy seeing their hard work smashed.

Another lovely Hispanic tradition is to serenade the birthday child in the morning with a special birthday song, *Las Mañanitas*.

Las Mañanitas

ña- na   en que ven- go a   sa- lu-   dar- te.

Ve-   ni- mos to-dos con gus- to   y pla-

cer   a   fe- li- ci-   tar- te.   *1. Ya   vie-   ne a-

ma- ne- cien- do,   ya la   luz del   día nos

dío.   Le-ván-   ta- te   de ma-   ña- na,

mi- ra   que ya a   ma- ne-   cío.

Verse 2:   El día en que tu naciste, nacieron todas las flores. En la pila del bautismo,
cantaron los ruiseñores.

Verse 3:   Quiesiera ser un San Juan, quisiera ser un Pedro y venirte a saludar con la
musica del cielo.

Verse 4:   De las estrellas del cielo, tengo que bajarte dos, una para saludarte, y otra
para decirte adiós.

Chorus 2:   Con claveles y jazmines te venimos a alabar por ser día de tu santo, te quer-
emos felicitar.

* Sing chorus number 1 with verse 1, 2 and 3, then sing verse 4 and end with chorus 2.

Translation: These are the morning songs that King David used to sing. Today because it is your saint's day, we sing them to you. Awake, my dear, awake. See how it is already sunrise. Already the birds are singing. The moon has tucked itself away.

Verse 1:   How lovely is the morning in which we come to greet you. We all come with pleasure to wish you happiness.

Verse 2:   On the day you were born all of the flowers were born, in your baptismal font the songbirds sang.

Verse 3:   I would like to be St. John, I would like to be St. Peter and come to greet you with the music of the heavens.

Verse 4:   Of the stars in the heaven I must send you two, one to greet you and one to say good-bye.

Chorus 1:   Already the day is dawning, already the day gives us its light. Rise up with the morning! See how it is already sunrise.

Chorus 2:   With carnations and jasmine, we came to praise you because it is your saint's day, we want to wish you happiness.

On birthdays, the child's unique personality shines forth. I will never forget Elly's fourth birthday. I had suggested Pin the Tail on the Donkey. "No!" she cried, "I don't want to hurt the donkey!" Elly has always had a great love of animals, and she wanted her birthday celebration to be a celebration of endangered species. We made pictures of these animals to hang about the room and gave out endangered-species stickers. Elly also insisted that there be no prizes for games unless everyone got a prize. She didn't want anyone to lose and feel bad on her birthday. These values were uniquely Elly's. As parents we think of ourselves as teaching our children values, but frequently they teach us. Each of our children has had something to teach us. Even a very young child can have strong beliefs and values. The birthday celebration gives your child's budding personality an opportunity to express itself fully.

Another birthday tradition from my family would have particular appeal to children from large families. There are five children in our family and on our birthday we got to go out to dinner to a restaurant of our choice with Mom and Dad. *Just* Mom and Dad. No Dwight, Phil, Chris or John. I remember we went to a restaurant one year at Jack London Square (*The Call of the Wild* was my favorite book at the time), and I had a huge bowl of red clam chowder (Mom's chowder was always white) and we talked about the chowder and about Jack London and about how cute I was as a baby. I felt very grown-up and very special.

It can be difficult for humans of any age to grasp that the glory of another person in no way lessens one's own glory. One way to begin teaching this basic lesson, while avoiding upset on a day meant to be joyful, is to give young siblings a small gift on their brother or sister's birthday. Gifts don't need to be expensive. They need to be thoughtful. We have all received presents that were so contrary to our own tastes and interests, they make us realize how little the gift-giver knows us. Most of us have also received presents that were deeply pleasing though not expensive. Our consumer society encourages us to buy people's love, or to prove our love through extravagance. We don't really want to teach our children that love can be bought and sold. A birthday is a time to say "You're special and we love you" in as many fun, silly, creative ways as you can think of.

Birthdays can be a particularly important and difficult time for children whose parents are divorced. Many children of divorce see their family differently than their parents do. For them, the internal reality is that everyone they love is family, whether or not they live in the same house. It can be helpful for children to have opportunities to experience externally what they see internally. Children often want their parents to get back together again. The parents know this isn't possible and may be afraid of doing things that might intensify the child's desires to get them back together. For this reason and because of the awkwardness and discomfort they feel when together, they may avoid coming together for celebrations that include everyone the child sees as family. For some couples it isn't feasible, emotionally or physically, to get together for the child's birthday. If this is the case, parents are wise to avoid making the child's birthday a stressful time. But for some couples it is possible to celebrate the child's birthday together in a positive way, and this can be a healing experience for the child. Make a rule, agreed on beforehand, that you won't discuss business or touchy subjects. Keep the focus off your differences and on your joy and pride in your child.

Vacations and Pilgrimages

We fantasize about vacations, much as we fantasize about holidays. We imagine relaxing, peaceful, fun-filled times when the family enjoys one another and everyone gets along. As Christian parents, we want to have family time that heightens our sense of togetherness. We want opportunities to be refreshed and renewed, not only as individuals, but as a family. I recall one time when I talked my husband and kids into going camping in Oregon. This was the sight of my favorite childhood vacations and I looked forward with excitement to sleeping in my husband's arms under the stars at night, taking a fishing boat out onto the lake, cooking the fish over a fire at night, singing around the campfire with the children and roasting marshmallows.

Now, I knew my husband wasn't a camper; he's a city kid who thinks roughing it is a Motel 6. I was confident, however, that the starlight on the lake and the fresh air would win him over. I couldn't have been more wrong. I felt at peace and energized; he was cold, uncomfortable and miserable. I could have fished for hours and cared less if I'd caught anything; he considered the fish's lack of interest a personal affront. I won't go into the gory details, but it was not long after he threw the fishing pole into a tree that we gave it up, packed up and headed for the nearest lodge. We ended up enjoying a good vacation, but it was hardly the vacation of my dreams.

There are a million reasons why it is difficult for family vacations to live up to our expectations. It is difficult, if not impossible, to satisfy the interests and tastes of every family member, so compromise becomes necessary. Family vacations can be hard to schedule, and the more family members there are, the more difficult scheduling becomes. Vacations can be expensive and put a strain on the family budget. Parental nerves can be further strained by the difficulty of traveling and eating out with young children. Starting with realistic expectations, keeping it simple and being willing to adapt can help make the family vacation an enjoyable time.

Vacations do not need to be expensive. Some of our best vacations have been mini-vacations where we went away for the weekend to a quiet little town. I remember one year we decided to stay at home (we were living in San Francisco at the time) and pretend we were tourists. We drove to Sausalito and took the ferry into San Francisco, ate at the wharf, took the cable car and shopped in Chinatown. It was a great day, and we saw our hometown through different eyes.

Vacations can be a good time to get together with family members or friends you enjoy. It is well worth developing such relationships when possible. We still reminisce fondly about the vacation we took with Uncle Bob, Aunt Janetha and our niece, Jenny. By pooling our resources, their family and ours were able to rent a houseboat on Lake Mead and a small motorboat for water-skiing. As we needed to pay for no other accommodations or entertainment and were able to cook on the boat, it turned out to be a relatively inexpensive vacation, and one of the most relaxing we've ever had.

Each family was responsible for a certain night's food and entertainment. We hosted a pirate night (à la the Pirates of the Caribbean) complete with eye patches, plastic daggers, a treasure hunt and walking the plank (into Lake Mead). They did an Hawaiian night with leis, a slurpy rendition of *aloha oi* on the tape recorder and a houseboat luau. It sounds silly, and it was silly. It was also fun, and it gave our families an opportunity to grow even closer. Strengthening extended family ties in this way can make your family life much richer and give your children an enlarged experience of support and belonging. Now that our children are teenagers and want to have more independence, they naturally turn to their aunts and uncles for a listening ear and advice. I can't think of anyone I'd rather have them turn to.

Most families take vacations together, but few make pilgrimages anymore. Yet there was a time when pilgrimages were extremely popular among Christians. A vacation is usually thought of as a time to get away from something; a pilgrimage is a time to go toward something. Going on pilgrimage seems to be a deeply rooted human instinct. Primitive pagans visited holy wells and trees. The Greeks visited the oracles of Delphi and Dodona. A pilgrimage to Mecca is a ritual obligation for Muslims, and Jews return to Jerusalem, as do Christians.

By the first century, it was already customary for Christians to make pilgrimages to the graves of martyrs, sometimes spending the night in prayer at their tombs. In the seventh century, pilgrimages became very popular. In the Middle Ages, the most popular destinations for pilgrimage were Santiago de Compostela (the shrine of St. James the Apostle) in northwest Spain, Rome and Jerusalem. The tomb of St. Nicholas in Bari, Italy, the shrine of the "Three Holy Kings" in Cologne and the sanctuary of St. Mary Magdalene in Provence were also popular.[6] The pilgrim received the Church's blessing before setting out, sometimes traveling barefoot. Pilgrims sewed cockle shells onto their hats if they were returning from Santiago, a pair of crossed keys or a replica of St. Veronica's handkerchief if returning from Rome and a palm leaf if returning from Jerusalem. Pilgrimages were sometimes penitential, but as often festive. Pilgrims rang little bells called Canterbury bells, sang songs and told stories, as did Chaucer's pilgrims in *The Canterbury Tales*.[7]

Today, Christian pilgrims may journey to Lourdes (where Mary appeared to Bernadette), Fatima (where she appeared to Lucia and Cousins) and Madjugorje (where she appeared to Croatian youth). Pilgrims visit the shrine of Our Lady of Guadalupe (who appeared to Juan Diego) in Mexico and to Our Lady of Knock in Ireland. Greek Orthodox Christians make pilgrimages to churches in Greece where the relics of saints are kept and to the sites where miracles have been performed. Thousands of pilgrims make their way to Aegina (where St. Nektarios is honored), Kerkyra, Corfu (where St. Spyridon is honored), the sacred Island of Patmos (where St. John wrote the book of Revelation), Tinos (honoring the Virgin Mary) and Simi (where a miraculous icon of St. Michael is housed).[8] If you are interested in making such a pilgrimage, you might want to look at Paul Higgin's book, *Pilgrimages: A Guide to the Holy Places of Europe for Today's Traveler* (Englewood Cliffs, NJ: Prentice-Hall, 1984) and Stewart Perowne's *Holy Places of Christendom* (New York: Oxford University Press, 1976).

What do people seek in these pilgrimages? Some seek healing from physical, emotional and spiritual ills. Some seek forgiveness, others insight. At heart, all pilgrims seek to feel a little closer to God by going to wherever God has been most visible. In addition to well-known holy sights, you might wish to visit the birth place of your patron saint or you might make a pilgrimage to the land of your family's roots. Connecting with our family history can give us insight into our own family and deepen our appreciation of our ancestors.

You do not need to go to Israel or Rome or the famous shrines to make a pilgrimage. What do you consider a holy place? It might be a church or a mountain or a lake. Many people make visits to their local cathedral or a local shrine. Some families visit the crèches set up at different churches at Christmas. Spend some time in your holy place. Light a candle. Say a prayer. Bring back a memento; it might be a leaf or flower to press or a medal to wear. I have a pressed leaf and a small green stone I brought back from a summer in Jerusalem on a shelf in my prayer corner. They remind me of the spiritual riches I uncovered there.

Whom do you consider a holy person? The person might be a saint, a teacher, a public figure or a friend. Read about the person's life. Visit a place where he or she lived. Seeing where someone lived and worked can make that person more real to us. If the person is living, write a letter. As a child I greatly admired C.S. Lewis and wrote him. I still have the letter he wrote in response.

I am writing this book a week after Cardinal Bernadin's death. My husband is Music Director at Holy Name Cathedral in Chicago, and our family has been much involved this last week in the music for the Cardinal's prayer vigil and funeral. The other night, as I came to the cathedral for choir rehearsal, I was amazed at the great numbers of people who had lined up outside the cathedral, waiting in the bitter November cold to pay their respects to this man, to see him one last time. Over 100,000 people came to view his body. Why did they come? I believe these people were on a kind of pilgrimage, seeking to come a little closer to God by being near a person in whom God was so visible. This is a natural human impulse, a deep, inner longing for the Eternal. When we go on pilgrimage, we allow holy places and holy people to influence us by their presence.

Sunday and Sabbath

In our busy, work-oriented culture, Sabbath may be the most neglected and most needed tradition of our rich spiritual heritage. Jesus, as an observant Jew, observed Sabbath, as did his first followers. Although he disagreed (as did many other Jews) with the regulation-minded attitude of the Pharisees toward the Sabbath, nothing suggests that he would have ignored the Sabbath. The creation story of Genesis

(Genesis 2:1-3) tells us that God rested on the seventh day from all his labors. The third commandment, "Remember the sabbath day, and keep it holy" (Exodus 20:8), instructs us to rest on the seventh day. Jesus teaches us that "the sabbath was made for humankind, and not humankind for the sabbath" (Mark 2:27). In the Letter to the Hebrews the author writes: "So then, a sabbath rest still remains for the people of God; for those who enter God's rest also cease from their labors as God did from his. Let us therefore make every effort to enter that rest" (Hebrews 4:9-11).

This Sabbath rest is not a mere cessation of activity, but rather a welcoming openness, suspended in time and space. Because the Jewish day begins in the evening, the Sabbath begins on Friday evening. At this time, the woman of the house kindles the Sabbath lights and says a special blessing. The family gathers, blessing and sharing the traditional hallah bread and kiddush cup of wine. A leisurely meal follows (traditionally one reclines on cushions while dining) and the night is filled with songs. Traditionally, Sabbath evening is the time of God's indwelling presence in the world when the family's ordinary activities (eating and drinking and sleeping) become sacred actions.[9] On Sabbath, our homes glow with a holy light from within.

Among the early Christians, there appear to have been two traditions connected with the Sabbath. On the morning of the Sabbath (Saturday), Christians gathered for a service of scripture and prayer like that practiced in the synagogue. On Saturday evening, they gathered again in one another's homes for a Sabbath meal where the Eucharist was celebrated (Acts 20:7). Christians began celebrating Eucharist on Sunday morning in the second century, and the liturgy of the Word (the Saturday morning service) and the liturgy of the Eucharist (the Saturday evening service) were combined.[10]

First century Christians called Sunday "the Lord's Day," a reference to Revelation 1:10 and probably a reference to the practice of celebrating the Lord's Supper on this day.[11] The day obtained its current title of Sunday from the Germanic people's pre-Christian worship of the sun. Sunday traditions involved gathering with other Christians to share God's word and presence in the Eucharist and resting in the ancient Jewish tradition of keeping the Sabbath holy, a day consecrated to God. Sunday as a day of rest became more widely observed in C.E. 321 when Emperor Constantine created a weekly holiday. In 789, Charlemagne prohibited work on Sunday on the grounds that it would violate the Sabbath. At the time of the Protestant Reformation, Sunday came to be known as the Sabbath, as the reformers tried to restore the sense of holiness original to the day. In Catholic tradition (according to Canon Law 1247), Christians are enjoined to abstain from business and labors that would inhibit the worship, joy and relaxation appropriate to the Lord's Day.[12]

My family were Sabbatarians and I have fond memories of our Sabbath family time. I remember leisurely meals, lots of singing and long drives in the country. (My father would always remind us that his father would not have bought gas on Sabbath and his father's father would not have driven a car on Sabbath.) My family has a strong Protestant work ethic, so this day of rest was quite a contrast and an important family time. As part of my own spiritual journey, I explored my family's Jewish roots, and began celebrating Sabbath Jewish style.

We decorate the dinner table with flowers, place a cloth (made by Elly) over our home-baked hallah (so it won't be jealous of the kiddush cup, which receives the first blessing). I kindle the Sabbath lights (two candles), singing *Baruch atah Adonai Eloheinu melech ha-olam asher kidshanu b'mitzvotav v'tzivanu l'hadlik ner shel shabbat.* (Blessed are you, Lord God, King of the universe who has sanctified us with His commandments and commanded us to kindle the Sabbath lights.) Sometimes our daughters join me in singing the blessing, using their own shabbat candles. We wish each other Shabbat Shalom. The kiddush cup (given to my husband by the synagogue where he used to work) is filled with grape juice and the kiddush is recited. Then we pray the blessing for the bread. In our home, the Sabbath meal is a time for song and laughter. (For Sabbath blessings and prayers, consult Central Conference of American Rabbis, *Gates of the House* [New York: Central Conference of American Rabbis, 1983].)

Hinei Mah Tov, a Sabbath Song

traditional Jewish

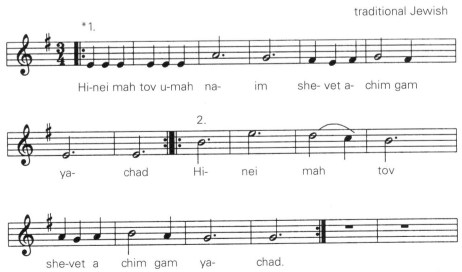

*Sing as a round, with the second voicing beginning when the first voice arrives at number 2.

Translation: How good it is and how pleasant, when brothers live as one.

(Psalm 133:1)

There are many wonderful Sabbath and Sunday traditions. In Germany and Belgium, "Sunday soups," often made with dumplings or meatballs, are traditional. In Italy and France, braised capon is traditional. In New England, brown bread and beans was the customary Sunday fare.[13] It is a Filipino tradition for families, including married children with their spouses and children, to meet at the parents' home for a family meal after Mass on Sunday. Before the meal, the children "kiss the hand" of their parents. The parents extend their right hands, which the child takes in his or her left hand. The child bows a little and puts the parents' hands to his or her forehead in a gesture of love and respect. This tradition helps families stay closely connected.

Sabbath Hallah

Combine 1 package (1 oz.) active dry yeast, 1 tablespoon sugar and 1/2 cup warm water. Let stand in warm place until it bubbles (about 10 minutes). In large bowl, sift together 4 cups flour and 3/4 teaspoon salt. Make a small well in the center.

In another bowl, beat 2 eggs (reserving approximately 1 tablespoon for later). Add to eggs, stirring:

> $1/4$ cup honey
> $1/4$ cup warm water
> $1/4$ cup vegetable oil
> prepared yeast mixture

Pour egg mixture into the well in your flour mixture, mixing well. Then knead on a floured board, adding enough flour to make elastic (not wet), approximately $1/2$ cup. Place dough in oiled bowl, cover with cloth and let rise in a warm place (approximately 1–2 hours).

Punch dough down, divide into three equal parts and roll into long ropes. Braid, pinching ends. (For a ring, pinch both ends together.) Place on a greased cookie sheet, cover with cloth again and let rise until double in size (approximately 30 minutes).

Preheat oven to 350 degrees. Brush top with remaining egg mixture mixed with a little water; sprinkle with poppy seeds. Bake for 30–40 minutes until golden brown.

First Communion

It has been the custom among many Christians to baptize infants and to receive Holy Communion for the first time around the age of seven. For centuries, children in many parts of Europe received first communion on the Sunday after Easter (also called the Octave of the Pasch). In many European countries, this Sunday was also called "Sunday in White" *(Dominica in Albis)*. It became traditional for those receiving First Communion on this day to dress in white, entering the church in a solemn procession with lighted candles. This tradition emphasized the connection between baptism and the reception of Communion. It was traditional in some communities for children to receive their first communion with their parents kneeling on either side of them.[14]

In Spain, children received first communion on December 8, the Feast of the Immaculate Conception. Houses were decorated with flowers and flags, and candles burned in the windows on the eve of the feast. In Seville, *Los Seises,* the Dance of the Six, was performed in the cathedral. Six young boys enacted a religious pageant before the Blessed Sacrament. It was traditional on this day for schools to have reunions. In South America, this was a day for school graduation ceremonies.[15]

In the United States, children still wear baptismal white for First Communion. At the Schools of the Sacred Heart, which our children attended, the girls wear garlands of white roses. Godparents, grandparents, family and friends join the child at church. Traditionally, the family gives a party afterward during which many of the foods traditional for baptism are served. This party declares that the Communion received at church must be lived and experienced in the community. The child's baptismal candle can be given a place of honor at the table and surrounded with flowers. Often guests bring special gifts, such as a rosary, prayer book, Bible or religious medal.

Be sure to take a picture and display it with the photos of other important life events (such as family weddings, birthdays and graduations). Another custom is for the child to make a banner that depicts his or her special religious interests or gifts. Talk with your children about what they value. Are they peacemakers? Do they have a thirst for justice? The banner can reflect these gifts and interests. Let the child make the banner out of felt and hang it in a place of honor.

First Communion Banner

Purchase a dowel approximately 3 inches longer than the width of the desired banner. Choose a medium-weight material of a solid color, such as broadcloth, for the banner and purchase a number of pieces of colored felt for the banner designs.

Cut the banner cloth into a rectangle the size you desire for your banner plus 4 inches in length and 2 inches in width. Hem the sides by folding fabric under 1/4 inch. Fold under another 3/4 inch. Press. Pin in place and stitch. Fold over the top 3 inches, turning under and pinning in place. Press and stitch close to the folded edge. The dowel will go through this end for hanging.

Have your child choose symbols that reflect his or her values. You might visit a church or look through books to get ideas for appropriate symbols or choose words that are important to your child, such as *justice, love* or *truth*. Make patterns by drawing your designs on paper, pin to colored felt and cut out. Arrange on banner, pinning in place. Stitch or glue onto the banner.

You might wish to trim the bottom of the banner with a decorative braid or fringe. Put banner on dowel. Tie string or ribbon to either end of the dowel and hang in a prominent place for your First Communion party.

Planting a Garden

Saint Fiacre once said, "One is nearer God's heart in a garden than anywhere else on earth." Perhaps the easiest way to help young people get in touch with the realm of the spiritual is to encourage them to step out of themselves and into nature. The power of the ocean, the quiet beauty of sunset, the stillness of trees and splendor of flowers speak eloquently of the Creator who is, perhaps, most visible in creation.

Throughout history, people have discovered God in the garden. God creates Adam and Eve to live in a garden paradise. Jesus used many images from the country in which he grew up. He used the mustard seed to teach us about faith and the lilies of the field to teach us about God's care for us. Jesus goes to the garden of Gethsemane to pray before his death, and when Jesus is risen from the dead, Mary mistakes him for a gardener. For centuries Christians have sought and discovered God in their gardens.

Planting a garden with your children can be great fun. It can help them experience God's creation in a very personal way and make the stories and images of scripture come alive for them. A garden can be a big project or a little one, an indoor garden or an outdoor one. Young children will take delight in something as simple as planting a seed in a small pot, putting it on the windowsill, watering it and watching for it to grow. To help children make the connection between the seed's growth and their own growth, measure the seedling and mark its growth just as you measure your child and mark your child's growth.

Whatever type of garden you plant, you and your children might wish to begin with a simple prayer.

Garden Blessing

Dear God, Creator of all that is good, bless this earth, these seeds of life, the hands that plant and weed, the water and sun that nurture. Help our garden to grow and help us to grow, day by day, in your grace. Amen.

Bean seeds grow easily and quickly. Read the parable of the seed (Matthew 13:1-9, 18-23) and tell your children that God has planted the Holy Spirit like a seed inside our hearts. (Say it simply and briefly, without turning it into a sermon.) Just as we nurture the plant with water, we nurture the seed of the Spirit by being good and loving and kind. When the plant sprouts, tell your children about the sprouts of spiritual growth you see in them. Make these affirmations specific, not general. "You were very patient with your little brother last night." "That was generous of you to offer to share your cookies." "I really respect you for telling the truth about breaking the lamp." "I was proud of you for studying so hard for that test." Such specific comments are worth so much more than a vague, "You're a good girl/boy." Take a picture of the plant and put it in the family album.

Grow plants you can eat or use. A vegetable garden or an herb garden gives children an opportunity to experience how God's creation provides for our needs: both our need to eat and our need for healing. Plant some that can be harvested quickly and others that will take a while. Most radishes can be picked in three weeks; spinach takes about forty days. Beans are easy to grow and mature rapidly. If space is limited you might try mini-varieties, such as Golden Midget sweet corn or Tom Thumb midget lettuce. Carrots and tomatoes are easy to grow. Let the children eat the food off the vine (it tastes best that way) and use some of the plants you have grown for meals. For fun, grow your own popcorn, peanuts or sunflowers. Try growing edible flowers for summer salads, such as nasturtiums, basil, lemon balm, rosemary and sweet marjoram.

Grow and harvest healing herbs to be used when a family member is ill. Garlic (high in vitamin C) and sage (use moderately for colds and sore throats) can be added to sauces and soups. Borage (in small amounts for reducing fever), chamomile (to relax), and mints (to refresh and aid digestion) can be used in teas.[16]

Learn about scripture by planting a Biblical Garden, a tradition from the Middle Ages. Plant rose of sharon and lily of the valley (Song of Solomon 2:1), crocuses (Isaiah 35:1), and lilies (Song of Solomon 2:16 and Matthew 6:28). Both lilies of the valley and daylilies are hardy. Plant mustard (Matthew 13:31) or any of the many herbs mentioned in scripture.

Rue (Luke 11:42) was grown in ancient Mediterranean lands by the Greeks and Romans. It grew in the gardens of Charlemagne and was used medicinally in the Middle Ages and the Renaissance. Called the "herb of grace," it was sprinkled over the faithful in the "asperges" ceremony at the beginning of the Mass.[17] "Hyssop," mentioned in John 19:29, is our marjoram (*origanum mara*), and garlic (Numbers 11:5), a member of the lily family, has long been valued for its healing powers. For centuries, it was thought to ward off evil.

Historically, spike or herbal vervarin (*verbena officinalis*) has been considered one of the most sacred of plants. It was considered a sacred plant among the Druids, a plant of the priest of Thor in Scandinavia, and used to brush the altars of the gods in Greece and Rome. It was called *Hierobotane*, or "holy plant," by the Greeks and *Herba Sacra*, or "sacred herb" by the Romans.

There are biblical references to the herbs mandrake (Genesis 30:14), coriander (Exodus 16:31), mint (Luke 11:42), cumin (Isaiah 28:25-27), dill (Matthew 23:23) and saffron and cinnamon (Song of Solomon 4:14). There are numerous biblical references to the olive (Jeremiah 11:16), the cedar (1 Kings 6:36), pine (1 Kings 6:33), willows (Psalm 137:2), wheat (Luke 22:31) and grape vines (Deuteronomy 20:6).

Learn about the lives of the saints by planting a Saint's Garden. A medieval Saint's Garden might have been planted in the shape of a cross with statues of Mary and other saints. Saint's Gardens contained lots of herbs and such flowers as lilies, roses, daisies, iris, violets, peonies, marigolds and dianthus. Often the Saint's Garden was enclosed, calling to mind the Song of Solomon (4:12), "A garden locked is my sister, my bride, a garden locked, a fountain sealed." These gardens often contained a shrine to a particular saint. Mary Gardens were particularly popular, and many plants came to be associated with her. Sweet-smelling branches from these gardens were strewn on the church floor for baptisms, weddings and funerals; sweet woodruff, thyme and rosemary were added to oriental gums to be burned as incense at the Mass. Violas, called *Herba Trinita* in the Middle Ages, are planted in the garden as a symbol of the Trinity, for this plant has three colors but one sweet smell. Here are some other saints with the plants associated with them:

Saint's Gardens

St. Agnes, Christmas rose

St. Paul, winter hellebore

St. Bride, dandelion

St. Margaret of Cortona, daisy

St. David, patron saint of Wales, leek

St. Patrick, Ireland's patron saint, the shamrock (another symbol of
the Trinity)

St. Joseph, white lilies and canterbury bells

St. Benedict, valerian, often called Herba Benedicta

St. Robert, wild geranium

St. Athanasius, tansy

Erasmus, scarlet pimpernell

St. Columba, barberry

St. Basil, basil

St. John, St. John's wort, larkspur and vervain

St. Peter, coxcomb and cowslip

Mary Magdalene, costmary

St. Anne, camomile, symbol of humility

St. Luke, marigold

St. Catherine, peaches

St. Barbara, St. Barbara's cress

Chrysanthemums are associated with the shepherds; Our Lady's bedstraw, penny-royal and thyme are manger herbs. You might want to decorate your nativity with these herbs at Christmas. Rosemary, the herb of remembrance, is also associated with the Holy Family's flight into Egypt. The white flower of the columbine resembles a white dove and signifies the Holy Spirit. Sage, or *salvia,* was used medicinally and is a symbol of salvation and immortality. Roses and lilies have usually been considered Mary's flowers.[18]

In your Saint's Garden, you might include a statue or garden plaque remembering St. Fiacre, the patron saint of gardeners. St. Fiacre was born in Scotia (now Ireland), became a monk and traveled to France, where he established a wilderness retreat in the district of Meaux. Here he grew herbs for healing and flowers for beauty. St. Fiacre became famous both for his healing herbs and for his wisdom, and people sought him out in his retreat. St. Francis, known for his love of nature, is often included in the Saint's Garden, along with St. Ambrose, the patron of beekeepers; St. Lawrence, protector of vineyards and patron of cooks; and St. Dorothea of the fruits and roses.

Other garden saints include: St. Giles, known as the patron saint of the woodlands and of all wounded animals; St. Isidore, the patron saint of farmers; and St. Phocas, patron in Greece of gardens and gardening, who spent his waking hours in prayer and the cultivation of his garden. St. Serenus of Greece lived an ascetic life in his garden, and St. Thérèse of Lisieux, the Carmelite contemplative, is called the Little Flower because of a love canticle she wrote. "To strew flowers is the only means of proving my love," she writes, "and these flowers will be each work, each daily sacrifice...I will spend my heaven doing good upon the earth, I will let fall a shower of roses."[19] Celebrate St. Thérèse's feast (October 3) by giving roses to the people you love and saying prayers for their well-being (or really get into the spirit of the feast and do this for the people who annoy you).

The story of St. Elizabeth of Hungary can be particularly inspiring to children, for she did so much at such a young age. Tradition tells us that she practiced acts of charity from the cradle, and was betrothed, as was customary in those times, at 4 years of age. She was married at the age of 14 to Ludwig IV. They had a very happy marriage, but a brief one. Ludwig went to fight in the crusades and was killed. Many of the people in power resented Elizabeth's charity and tried to put a stop to it.

Elizabeth, undeterred, put loaves of bread into her apron and stole out of the castle to feed the starving people. While descending the castle steps, she was stopped by the castle steward and his men. When they asked what she was carrying, she told them that she was only carrying roses. One of the men grabbed hold of her apron and there fell from it fragrant rose petals. A cross of brilliant light, the story goes, appeared over her head. She continued to feed the poor, with fish she caught herself, and to clothe the poor with garments she made herself until she died at the tender age of 24. If you dedicate a section of your garden to St. Elizabeth, you might want to make herb bread on her feast day (November 19) to give to a homeless shelter or soup kitchen.

Herb and Olive Focaccia

Dissolve 1 package dry yeast (1 oz.) and 1/2 teaspoon sugar in 1 cup warm water. Set in warm place for about 10 minutes until mixture bubbles. Add, stirring thoroughly:

    1 teaspoon salt

    3 tablespoons olive oil

    2 $\frac{1}{2}$ cups flour

Knead on floured board for several minutes. Place in oiled bowl, turn to cover with oil, cover bowl with damp cloth and set in warm place to rise. Dough should double in bulk (about 40 minutes).

Turn dough onto greased baking sheet, punch down and spread with fingers or rolling pin into rectangle (about 1/2 inch thick). Brush with olive oil. Make indentations with fingers and put in black pitted olives. Sprinkle with 1 tablespoon fresh thyme, chopped, and 1 tablespoon fresh rosemary or oregano.

Bake in preheated oven at 450 degrees for 30 minutes. To give bread a good crust, mist with water two times in first 10 minutes of baking.

It is traditional among many Polish and Czech-Americans in Iowa and Minnesota to bring their kitchen herbs and spices to church for the priest's blessing on the morning of the Feast of the Assumption (August 15). The scripture reading for this feast is from Sirach 24:15: "Like cassia and camel's thorn I gave forth perfume, and like choice myrrh I spread my fragrance."[20] Among Polish Americans, the Blessed Mother is honored on the Feast of the Assumption under her title of Our Lady of the Flowers. In Poland and in many Polish American communities, the harvest wheat festival is held on this day. The people bring bouquets of flowers and bags of seed for next year's harvest to morning Mass for blessings. Children bring flowers, an apple and a carrot to be blessed and then place these in the attic.

According to some, this protects the house from lightning.[21] You might decorate your home with bouquets of lilies and roses or with bowls of rose potpourri in honor of Mary on the Feast of the Assumption.

Attract butterflies, a symbol of the resurrection, to your garden by planting ageratum, clematis, cosmos, daylilies, hollyhocks, lobelia, marigolds, nasturtium, phlox, salvia, verbena or zinnias. Each stage of the butterfly's life represents the stages of the Christian life: The crawling caterpillar represents our mortal life on earth; the cocoon, when the chrysalis appears lifeless, depicts the body in the grave (Christ in the tomb); at last, the emerging butterfly represents the resurrected Christian.

Share the joys of your garden with the people you love by making gifts from your garden for Christmas, birthdays or namedays. Strawflowers, statice, baby's breath, roses, heather, lavender, sunflowers and yarrow are all good for drying and can be made into long-lasting flower arrangements. To dry flowers, pick them on a sunny, dry day, tie in bunches together and hang upside down in a cool, dry room. Arrange in a basket with floral foam wired to the bottom.

Make potpourris and sachets of sweet-smelling petals and herbs. These can be placed in drawers with clothing or in closets, or put in a dish to scent a room. Pick flowers, herbs and citrus peels and dry them by spreading in thin layers on screens in a dark place. When completely dry, put in an airtight container and store in a cool dry place. Experiment with different mixtures to create your own recipe. For sachets, trim circle of attractive cloth with lace, fill with a sweet petal and herb mixture and tie with a ribbon.

Potpourri Recipes

Mix together:

- 1 cup rose petals
- 1 cup lavender
- $1/4$ cup rosemary
- $1/2$ cup granulated orris root
- a few drops lavender or rose oil
- cinnamon sticks, cloves and
  powdered nutmeg *(optional,*
  makes a spicier scent)

For a clean, fresh-smelling potpourri, mix together:

- 2 cups lemon verbena
- 1 cup lemon balm
- $1/2$ cup rose geranium petals
- 1 cup orange mint leaves
- $1/2$ cup grated lemon peel
- 2 teaspoons granulated orris root
- a few drops lemon oil

For a mixture to repel insects from
your good woolens, mix together:

tansy	wormwood	lavender	rue or vetiver
clary sage	santolina	pennyroyal	lemon balm

When we celebrate the special days and holy days of our family life, we mark not the passing of time but our growth within that time. When we name, own and affirm our growth, it becomes easier to keep growing—we are encouraged by the constant presence and work of the Spirit.

The child I nursed not so long ago will be leaving for college soon. How fast they grow up! Let us use our time well, to grow in love and faith, for time passes quickly and our children need deep roots, sunlit hearts and cultivated minds.

7

Loving the Adolescent: Letting Go Doesn't Mean Giving Up

Not long ago another choir member and I were happily discussing the merits of our respective children as we made our way back to the music room following morning services. "It's so good to hear a mother of teenagers say something nice about her children!" my friend said. Her children are 2 and 4 years old. "I look at my little ones and wonder, will they turn into these monsters everyone complains about?"

Adolescents get a bad rap in our society, a highly peculiar attitude in view of the fact that our culture simultaneously idolizes youth. My children are now 14 and 16, and I've never enjoyed them more. My appreciation of adolescents is not, I assure you, rooted in inexperience or naiveté. I specialized for many years in working with addicted and dual diagnosis adolescents and their families. These were the kids who were getting high, cutting class, running away, committing crimes, joining gangs, and generally driving the adults around them crazy. With help, most of these kids turned their lives around and proved themselves to be delightful people with a great deal to offer others.

When people asked me what I did for a living and I explained that I worked with teenage drug addicts, the inevitable response was, "Why on earth would you want to do that?" The truth is that I like working with adolescents, even the troubled ones, because they are exciting and interesting, idealistic and courageous. Adolescence is a difficult, challenging, but exciting time of life when the young adult begins to leave the security of home and family and find his or her own way in the greater world. Because adolescents often begin this journey with strong emotions, intense idealism and intoxicating dreams, these years have the potential to be a profoundly spiritual time of life.

Why is it, then, that our youth-oriented culture is so down on adolescents? I believe our negative attitude is connected to our idealization of youth. The idealization of a segment of society historically accompanies their oppression. Women, for example, were placed on a pedestal and called the moral conscience of society at the same time that they were denied the right to vote and refused equal pay for equal work. Blacks were often considered noble savages, admired for their great rhythm and emotionalism, while simultaneously being denied the right to respect and individualism. Native Americans were extolled for their affinity with the Earth, yet their lands were taken from them. These attitudes persist. In a similar way, our culture admires youth but, to a large degree, denies young people a viable and significant role in society, gives them the short end of the stick when it comes to medical care, and routinely subjects them to prejudice.

The rite of passage of adolescence is the rite of initiation. Certain traditional aspects of this rite are particularly important. The rite involves some sort of quest, or a journey of self-discovery, an affirmation by the adult community and a welcoming into that community as an equal and valued member. Through this process, the adolescent passes out of childhood and into adulthood. Our culture has few rites of initiation to guide the young person on this journey. In our society, car keys, beer and cigarettes symbolize adulthood. Without other, more meaningful rites, is it any wonder that so many of our young people rely heavily on drinking, smoking and driving to prove themselves adults?

This is a serious problem, for we desperately need our youth to play a real and essential role in our society, just as we needed youth to play a critical role in the growth of our faith. Recall that Mary was probably an adolescent when she said "yes" to the angel at the annunciation and Jesus was an adolescent when he declared his independence, went to teach in the temple and told his parents, in true adolescent fashion, that he must be about his Father's business.

When we think of adolescent rites of passage, we are likely to think of such practices as the vision quests of the Sioux. The Sioux used dreams for guidance. In the vision quest, the adolescent Sioux would go out and seek dreams or visions to guide him in adult life. He would venture out into the prairie, unarmed and naked, humbly asking God for guidance. Select members of his tribe would help him to interpret his dream and encourage him to pursue and excel as a hunter or warrior, priest or medicine man.[1] This was a deeply spiritual process, and simultaneously, a profoundly practical one. Encouraged to open up to the divine and seek his innermost dreams, the youth then received careful guidance from the adults of his culture. He emerged from the process with an adult role to play in his society. Our culture has no equivalent, although many Christians are attempting to address these needs.

Some Christians in the African American tradition have been creating rites of passage for adolescents. In the early 1960s, Ron Karenga visited Kenya and Tanzania, where he observed the Harvest Festival of Swahili-speaking tribes. From these people, he learned the *Nguzo Saba*, or "Seven Values." These are expressed in *Kiswahili*, a nontribal language developed to enable people of different language backgrounds to communicate with each other. The principles of Nguzo Saba have been adapted by Christian African Americans to resonate with Christian beliefs and used to develop positive spiritual identity among African American youth.[2]

One such effort is the Boyhood to Manhood program for African American youths, ages 7 through 12. This program provides young people with a rite of passage experience emphasizing cultural heritage, biblical study, family values and community involvement. Relationships with mentors encourage emotional development. Reflections, discussions and activities help the young person better understand his body, sexuality and health needs, as well as his emotional and spiritual development. The final session is an initiation ceremony in which the young person is acknowledged to be an adult in a ritual that is both joyful and solemn. The initiation ceremony is followed by a feast with African and soul food, music and dancing.[3] Such new traditions can powerfully inspire and guide our young people when they are authentic. That is, we as Christians must make sure that these young people are journeying *into* something, that they are given work worthy of their abilities and opportunities worthy of their dreams, that they are entering a community that will continue to support them.

Look for opportunities to create traditions within your family or community that will acknowledge your young person's growth and maturity. You might give your daughter a gift or cook a special meal on the day her menstruation begins. This can be done simply and privately so as not to embarrass her, but it is an important event and should be acknowledged. A son's first shave could also be acknowledged. We make our daughters' 16th birthdays special by giving them each one of their great-grandmother's rings. They have known since they were little and liked trying on Mama's jewelry and clothes that they would receive one of these rings when they turned 16. It is a simple way to say "You are growing up" and "You are special."

In the Filipino community, a young woman's 18th birthday serves as a rite of passage. A debutante ball is given and she is presented to family and friends. The father dances with his daughter and gifts are given. In the Philippines she wouldn't be allowed to go to parties until this event. In the U.S., this event is more likely to take place when the girl is 16, in keeping with American "sweet sixteen" traditions. Here in Chicago, churches may make the party arrangements for groups of adolescents. Parents pay the church for providing these services.

Examine your adolescent's life and make time to celebrate his or her interests. Try having one night a week as a designated "friend" night when you encourage your children to invite their friends for dinner. Or invite your child's best friend and his or her family for dinner. Most young people dream of what they will be when they grow up. Enter into these dreams. Does your daughter want to be an astronaut? Take a trip to the Smithsonian or your local science museum. Does your son want to be an artist? Attend your local art galleries. A mathematician? Give a medal of the patron saint of mathematics. Do they want to go to a particular college? Try to visit that school with them. Give them gifts, take trips, introduce them to people and experiences that relate to their interests and dreams. Honor their accomplishments. Bring bouquets of flowers to their recitals and plays (even young men can appreciate this). Order a celebration pizza when their team wins or they get a ribbon at a science fair.

In our family, education is important, so we make a big deal out of graduations. For our daughters' eighth grade graduations we sent them to Ireland to spend the summer with my husband's sister and her family. In this way we celebrated their accomplishments, acknowledged their growth, and gave them an opportunity to experience the world beyond our neighborhood and immediate family.

In 1972, the American bishops in the Latin tradition decided that early adolescence was the proper age for confirmation, so confirmation is sometimes called the "sacrament of Christian maturity."[4] St. Thomas teaches that "age of body does not determine age of soul."[5] Confirmation is associated, not with physical, but with spiritual maturity. It is the fruition of the grace received in baptism. Practically speaking, it is a time for the child who has reached the age of reason to claim the faith of his or her upbringing.

During the first four centuries, there was no uniformity in Christian initiation rites. When it became customary to baptize infants soon after birth, it was not always possible for the bishop to be present for the special anointing that only the bishop can perform, so this part of the ritual was often delayed. By the 5th century, this ritual had come to be known as confirmation. During the 9th through 13th centuries the tradition spread throughout Europe. Children were often confirmed before the age of 2 years.

In modern times, confirmation normally occurs during adolescence. Young people prepare for confirmation through a period of study, prayer and acts of charity. The young person selects the name of a saint whom he or she wishes to emulate. This saint becomes the child's patron. In some families parents write letters to their child, offering these words of blessing and affirmation to the child during the service. The rite of confirmation is administered by anointing the forehead with sacred chrism (oil), with the laying on of hands by the bishop, and the words: "Be sealed with the Gift of the Holy Spirit."[6] It is traditional for family and friends to gather after the confirmation for a party. For our daughter's confirmation we decorated the dining table with flowers and set out her baptismal candle. It is a Portuguese tradition to serve *Massa Sovada*, a sweet bread, at confirmation, to symbolize the Holy Spirit.[7]

Confirmation or any other initiation rite must be accompanied by a change in how the young person is treated. This can be a progressive series of changes rather than a single overnight one. Your children's confirmation or passage through a rite of initiation is an acknowledgment that they have reached a certain level of spiritual maturity; they should be treated accordingly. They will continue to need our guidance and support, but now they also need to know that we trust their ability to make decisions and act responsibly. We must be prepared to give them responsibilities and privileges appropriate to their new status as mature Christians. This may involve such simple everyday things as letting them choose their own bedtime, extending their curfew, or asking them to help with more adult duties in the home. You might also ask the adolescent to take on a different, more mature role in family traditions and religious practices. You might invite the adolescent to lead family prayers or to take a more important role in preparing holiday decorations and meals.

As parents, we need to visibly acknowledge in our own behavior that our children are growing up. This will be easier for some of us than for others, either because we are more or less protective, or because our children are more or less mature. Letting go begins when our children are still little. We let go of our children's hands when they are able to safely cross the street themselves. We let go when we let our children choose for themselves what clothes they are going to wear. There are a million little ways in which we let go and let them grow. It is a familiar process for us, but somehow it is harder when our children are adolescents. Perhaps it is harder because we know that if they stumble now, they will have farther to fall and greater chances of getting hurt.

Perhaps these times are hard because we know our children will soon fly farther from the nest. Some parents look forward to this, but many parents fear this time in their child's life. Many parents are afraid that their child's independence somehow translates into a lack of love for their family. I have worked with families where the children were loved and well cared for, and I have worked in families where the children were abused by their parents. Children from both families continue to have a strong sense of attachment to and need for their parents. To the parents who fear adolescence, I would say that the bond between you and your child is stronger than you know. If you have taught your children well, you have every reason to trust that they will live good and holy lives; but inevitably, the choice is theirs, not ours.

In my own experience, this letting go is mutual and gradual, but it is far from a smooth process. It better resembles the fits and starts of a driver just learning to shift gears than a smooth automatic cruise control. There are times when my children treat me as if I were suddenly anathema. They would rather spend time with almost anyone other than me and they seem to consider my ideas and habits quaint, even amusing. At other times they climb onto my lap or want me to fix them hot cocoa or want me to listen as they tell me all about an experience they've just had. They love me to tell them stories from their childhood and want my opinion on the colleges and careers they are considering. The difficulty comes from never knowing which mood they are going to be in. But then, they probably don't know either.

I think transitions are like this for all of us at any age. At one moment we are ready to take on the world, and a few moments later we want to crawl back into the warm, safe womb. Most of us, when we are in transition, find comfort in having a safe and stable port. I think parents need to try to provide that safe, stable place for their children. It isn't always easy to do, for we are often going through changes in our own lives, but our children need and deserve consistency, stability, patience and unconditional love. At such a time, the traditions of childhood become a firm framework on which to hang one's ever-changing life.

I found out just how important these traditions still were to my daughters when we were packing before our recent move to the Midwest. I wanted to throw away a dilapidated old Advent calendar. "No!" they cried, as if I were about to commit some sort of sacrilege. The crib quilts, the family joke book, the prayer book we made when they were little, the hallah cover Elly made in third grade, their first communion banners, all had to come with us. In a few years, they will be embarking on a greater adventure. College, marriage, children of their own, careers, a whole wide world of challenges and opportunities lies before them. They will carry with them all the little traditions we have lived together over the years. I trust that these traditions will give them a measure of security as they enter into the many changes and unknowns that lie ahead.

8

Aging and Dying: The Not-So-Empty Nest

The focus of this book has been on starting and building young families, but as life expectancy increases, today's young families are frequently called on to rear the young while caring for the elderly. Furthermore, with more two-income and single-parent families, many young parents turn to the grandparents to take on significant parenting responsibilities for their grandchildren. It is not really possible, therefore, to address the needs of young families without some discussion of aging and the importance of healthy interaction between generations.

Many cultures revere the elderly and honor them for their wisdom and experience, but our culture all too often makes the elderly feel devalued and useless. Elderly people may find themselves ignored or dismissed by salespeople and professional people (such as physicians, even ministers) or patronized by people half their age. I recall going shopping with my grandmother, a bright, active woman. She would begin to tell the saleswoman what she wanted, and the saleswoman, ignoring her, would turn to me and ask me what my grandmother wanted. Needless to say, we promptly left the store. This happened frequently, and yet it never ceased to amaze and anger me. Clearly this is not a Christian approach to aging.

We need to be sure that the elderly members of our families know that we value and respect them. We show this respect in concrete ways: by staying in touch rather than ignoring or abandoning our elderly; by being open to learn from them, rather than treating their input as irrelevant or outdated; and by caring for them as they once cared for us when they need our help.

Family traditions of reunion can help maintain contact between family members when the youngsters fly the nest. Generational traditions can provide opportunities for the wisdom and experience of older family members to be passed on to the young. Traditions of gratitude can help us be truly caring when we are called to care for elderly family members.

In our mobile society, the fabric of family life is easily fragmented. We need to make the time to keep in touch, so that our relationships with each other continue to grow and mature even if we are not living in the same house or the same state. Traditions of reunion help us maintain meaningful contact, enabling us to experience our family wholeness and holiness. We need to take time to think about how we can encourage this interaction in our own families.

Consider planning weekly, monthly or annual get-togethers. Of course many families gather on Thanksgiving or Christmas, but there are some advantages to creating family reunion days that are free of the stresses, secular expectations and commercialism of these holidays. You might try celebrating the Feast of the Holy Family. It wasn't until after the 16th century that devotion to the Holy Family became popular and not until 1920 that it was celebrated universally. This relatively modern feast day has a particular significance now as modern families struggle with so many challenges and changes. The feast is observed on the Sunday after Christmas. Many parish churches have special celebrations, inviting families to renew their commitment and love for one another on this day.[1] You might make this a day for family reunions, when the family attends church services together followed by a festive family meal. Take a multi-generational family portrait each year on this day.

When grandparents are hospitalized or require nursing home care, establish regular times for visiting and make it a priority for the family to visit together. Visiting day can be a fun day with a picnic atmosphere. Consider bringing games, school projects, children's artwork, photos and the like to share. You might want to pray together during these visits or arrange to receive Holy Communion together.[2]

Check with your children's school about having a Grandparent's Day. The Schools of the Sacred Heart, which our children attended, had a Grandparent's Day each year. Grandparents were invited (by the grandchildren) to attend school with them. Grandparents made every effort to attend, but if a child's grandparents couldn't attend, he or she got to adopt a friend's grandparent. Grandparents attended classes with their grandchildren, met the teachers, were honored at a special party and often took their grandchildren out to dinner afterwards. Both our children and our parents looked forward to this special event.

The book of Proverbs tells us that "Grandchildren are the crown of the aged" (Proverbs 17:6). We need to let the young benefit from the love and wisdom of the old, and the old benefit from the energy and innocence of the young. Young people need the love and guidance of older people, and older people need to be able to see the worth of their own lives reflected in what they pass on to the young. We are interdependent. In generational traditions members of the older generation serve as mentors, models and spiritual guides to the younger generation. Younger people need to ask for this mentoring and guidance and older people need to offer it.

Grandparents might invite their grandchild to spend an evening with them and teach them a skill. The skill could be anything: how to fix a leaky faucet, how to bake biscuits, how to tell a joke or how to crochet slippers. The grandparents can pick something they want to teach or the grandchildren could pick something they would like to learn. I know one woman who for Christmas one year wrote down what she alone knew about her family history. She had prints made of some old family photos and gave these histories and photos in a lovely book to each of her children and grandchildren.

There are many opportunities to become mentors and "honorary grandparents" in the community. I recall a program in California where people volunteered to be grandparents for young people who'd gotten into trouble with the law. The program brought together responsible adults with teenagers needing guidance. I heard of another program in New England in which a residential home for the elderly helped in the running of a day care for children. Many businesses now provide mentoring programs for schools, and most community organizations caring for children need volunteers. Invite elderly relatives or people in your community to share what they have to offer. The relationships that develop can be rewarding for both the adults and youngsters.

The fifth commandment (Exodus 20:12) requires that we honor our parents. Jesus reminds his followers (Mark 7:10-12) of this Jewish tradition of filial honor and duty. This tradition teaches us that to neglect our duty to our parents is to compromise our attitude toward life and to jeopardize our relationship with God. How can we dishonor those who gave us birth and reared us without distancing ourselves from our Creator? Filial duty involves caring for the physical needs of parents to be clothed, fed and housed, but it also involves treating parents with respect. Duty is not a popular word these days. Duty is often seen as cumbersome and inhibiting. People long to be "free " from duties, and yet the book of Sirach tells us that "those who honor their father atone for sins, and those who respect their mother are like those who lay up treasure" (Sirach 3:3-4). Whoever honors his or her parent, we are told, will be heard by God when he or she prays (Sirach 3:5).

We rarely think of gratitude as a powerful force in human affairs and yet Jesus, knowing the difficulties that would face his family and friends and wanting to prepare and strengthen them, called on the power of gratitude during the Last Supper, breaking bread and giving thanks. St. Paul tells us to "give thanks in all circumstances" (1 Thessalonians 5:18). In the traditions of gratitude we acknowledge our responsibility to honor our parents by showing them respect and by caring for their needs. We take on these responsibilities as an act of gratitude and an expression of thanksgiving for those who gave us life. Scripture tells us that these acts of thanksgiving are powerful, atoning for sins, making our prayer effective, enriching and expanding our lives. Caring for elderly parents can be a difficult and stressful job. It is easy to lose sight of the deeper meaning and spiritual power inherent in this caregiving. Traditions of gratitude help us uncover and remember this deeper meaning.

Traditions of honor and respect are often simple. Many Chinese and Vietnamese American families honor elderly parents by bowing before them on the first day of the new year, wishing them long life, prosperity and happiness. Filipino Americans visit their parents after Mass on Sunday and "kiss the hand" of the parent (placing the parent's right hand on their forehead) as a sign of respect. Serving Grandpa first at the dinner table or asking Grandma to give the blessing are other simple ways to show respect.

As a therapist I have come to believe that the surest way to show respect is by listening: listening with open and attentive minds, without interruption, without advice, without being compelled to correct or fix the other person's point of view. Attentive listening is simple, difficult and deeply spiritual. When do we take time to really listen to the elderly members of our family? Would it be possible to create traditions of listening?

Many cultures rely on the elderly to be the storytellers, passing on through their stories both the history of the family and insight into the family's beliefs and values. These storytelling traditions are traditions of listening. In Eskimo tradition, for example, it is in the Singing House that the elders tell the stories their elders told to them. Because they lacked a written language, the Eskimo relied on an oral tradition. Each generation listened to the story of its people, learned these stories by heart and passed them, through the ritual of storytelling in the Singing House, from generation to generation.[3]

There are many ways to encourage this storytelling. Have a storytelling night with grandparents as the guests of honor. Set a festive table, serve family recipes, ask the grandparents to give their blessing at the beginning of the meal to grown children and grandchildren. After dinner, bring out the family albums and sit together. The grandparents can tell family stories and talk about the pictures in the album. Sing the songs traditional to your family. If grandparents live at a distance, ask them to tell their stories in letters or on tape or by a conference call. I know of another family who had an inter-generational sleep over complete with ghost stories and junk food. They were surprised when the middle-aged parents were the first to fall asleep, while the grandparents and grandkids talked late into the night.

Grandparents might take their children or grandchildren to the house or town where they grew up. One year my family went with my grandfather to Whiskey Creek, Washington, where he lived as a child. He told us stories as we walked through the fields, describing the houses now gone, and the people who had once lived there. It was a powerful, poignant experience.

We need to foster communion between the generations, but we must also recognize that people of every age need personal space and privacy. When living space is limited, how do we respect each family member's need for personal space? I remember when my grandmother broke her hip and it was no longer feasible for her to live on her own. She was an independent woman who found this transition difficult. My parents expended considerable energy to build an apartment for her in our basement. In this way she maintained some independence even as she, of necessity, became more dependent. Not every family can do this. For some families, a separate room may be possible, or a separate space within a shared room.

Personal space is not always physical. Sometimes respecting personal space involves not using (or moving) another's things without permission, or respecting a person's different sense of time, letting a person take his or her time over a meal, for instance, without hurrying him or her along. Working with elderly people in the hospital, I found that the thoughtless moving and misplacing of an individual's personal belongings (a rosary, a book, a box of Kleenex) was a frequent and unnecessary source of irritation and a very concrete sign of disrespect. We all have our little rituals that define our personal sense of time and space. We need to respect these.

If you are caring for an elderly family member, it is easy to become isolated and overwhelmed. Isolation only increases the stress and difficulty of the task. It is important to reach out and utilize the support available in your community. Home nursing, lay visitors and church ministries to the elderly can provide much-needed support. Have an extended family conference and ask each family member what he or she can do to contribute to the care needed. Too often one family member ends up carrying the responsibilities that should be shared by all. If someone in your family is terminally ill, find out about hospice services. Hospice can be a wonderful resource, both medically and spiritually, for the family dealing with terminal illness.

Talk with elderly family members about their wishes regarding medical care at the end of life, life support, "extreme measures" and organ donation. Families are often afraid to talk about these issues, but such discussions, if respectfully and lovingly handled, can bring families closer together and make later decisions far easier. If you are uncomfortable discussing these issues, ask a therapist, chaplain or minister to help facilitate the discussion.

The issue of self-care, so important in child care, is also critical when it comes to caring for the elderly. Build traditions of self-care into your life. I have one friend who is caring for an elderly mother. For her, choir night is her time for renewal. Her sister cares for their mother on choir night. Honoring our parents does not mean that we should become so consumed by their needs that we fail to care for ourselves. Elder abuse often arises in high-stress situations when caregivers fail to meet their own needs. We are better able to respect others when we respect ourselves. If you are losing perspective on this, get a reality check from a competent third person.

From a spiritual perspective, life is never used up, never out of date, never meaningless. Life comes from God, continues in God and returns to God. Life is always meaningful, always valuable, always to be honored. Through traditions of reunion, generation and gratitude, we manifest our belief in the ongoing value of life. In so doing we enrich and validate the lives of others as well as our own.

There is a prayer in the Yom Kippur Liturgy, "Do not cast us out in our old age." The Ba'al Shem Tov, the founder of Hasidism, interpreted this as meaning: "Do not condemn us to days that are old, but rather help us make each day new."[4]

Traditions of Death and Mourning

Watching our parents, grandparents, great uncles and great aunts, and other family members approach the end of their lives is a powerful reminder of our mortality. Just as we reach middle age we witness our parents (who have *always* been middle aged to us!) move into their elder years. What a striking and forceful manifestation of the brevity of life!

Not long after my mother-in-law's death, I remember 2-year-old Teresa asking, "Who is caring for Grandma now?" Teresa had watched us nurse Grandma for many months as the cancer ravaged her body and mind. Though Grandma had died and gone to be with God, didn't she still need to be nursed and loved? "The angels are caring for Grandma," we told her, and Teresa seemed satisfied with that simple explanation.

Not long afterward, we all went to see the Vatican Art exhibit at the De Young Museum. In one room there was an immense oil painting of Jesus taken down from the cross. The angels were nursing his wounds. Teresa stopped in front of that painting and studied it silently for a long time. After we went on to the other rooms, she returned to that room to stand attentively in front of that painting. I realized that she was thinking about Grandma, remembering her thin, wounded body, imagining the angels nursing her in heaven as we had nursed her on Earth. I stood beside her, gazing at the painting, and we talked about Grandma for a while. We bought a book that contained a picture of this painting and for many months afterward, Teresa would take it off the shelf and look at this picture. I believe she found in this picture a way to remember Grandma, and a way to understand what had happened to Grandma.

We don't like to think about children when we think about death. We want to protect them from such things. Parents hesitate to tell children that someone is dying or has died. They avoid giving children information. Sometimes children are not permitted to view the body or to attend the funeral, and may be ignored by adults who are distraught or simply unwilling to acknowledge that children grieve. Often our efforts to protect children from death only isolate them. The fact is that children are aware of death and experience grief when someone they love dies. Their needs are not so different from our own.

Death is a natural part of life. When death was more likely to occur at home than in the hospital, when more people lived in an agricultural society where they saw plants and animals die and felt the direct impact of these deaths, it was impossible to grow up without knowing something about death. Nowadays, however, it is easy for a person to grow up with little contact with or experience of death.

It is helpful to have talked with our children about death before we are faced with an actual death. How do we talk to our children about death? Because death is a natural part of life, we encounter it naturally. The easiest way to approach the subject of death is to take advantage of these natural encounters. You see a dead bird on the sidewalk, a pet dies, there is a death in a story or a television show. Take time to notice. Let your child ask questions. Listen. Answer what you can, but don't be afraid not to have all the answers. No one has all the answers about death, and this is part of what your child needs to learn.

With young children especially, be concrete and avoid abstractions. Words like "immortality" mean little to a 5-year-old. Avoid euphemisms like "He's gone to sleep." Young children may take you literally and become afraid of what will happen when they go to sleep. Children are individuals and react differently to death. I have known children who dissolve in tears at the sight of a dead sparrow, and others who want to dissect it. Both children and adults need to be free to stand in their own truth: the truth of what they actually feel (not what they are "supposed" to feel or "shouldn't" feel).

Young children are likely to think of death as reversible and not permanent, like taking a trip or going to sleep. In fact, young children and spiritually mature saints bear a striking similarity to one another in their approach to death. Neither see death as permanent. Because young children have a limited understanding of death, adults expect them to be less affected by it. In truth, however, both those with little understanding and those with great understanding are equally moved by death.

Children may react to a loss within the family (and to changes in the behavior of the adults who care for them) with problems with sleeping or eating. They may cling to their parents, or become withdrawn. Children between 5 and 9 are more likely to understand the finality of death, but have difficulty realizing that it can happen to them. In fact, many adults as well as older children may regress to more childlike ways of thinking about death when confronted with the death of a loved one.

Some time ago I participated in a memorial service for those who had died during the year at the hospital where I work as a chaplain. At one point in the service, we read off the names of each person who had died. As we read the names, a family member came forward and was given a red flower in memory of the loved one.

After the service a small boy came up to me. He couldn't have been more than 5. "Look at this," he said proudly, holding out the red flower. "This is my Mommy's flower." He and I sat down for a while, and he told me about his mother. He told me that he felt sad and missed her, especially at night. He told me she liked flowers. I couldn't bring his mother back. I couldn't take away his pain or his tears; but I could listen. It seemed to be what he wanted. Often mourners do not need something done for them as much as they need someone to be with them.

Children need simple, honest information in response to their questions. The images and stories that our tradition offers us, such as the painting of Christ and the angels, can be as meaningful for children as for adults. Children need to be listened to, to have their emotions acknowledged and validated. They need to be included, not isolated, and to receive words and gestures of support and comfort from family and friends, to be able to talk about their experience and know that they are heard.

As Christians, we have many beliefs and traditions that help us deal with death. We have traditions that give death meaning and traditions that guide us through our grief. What we teach our children about death influences how they will face life. Death can teach us to value life, to not take our lives and our loved ones for granted. People who have worked through an experience of death or loss are often better able to face their fears with courage and inner peace.

What do we, as Christians, believe about the meaning of death? In the Hebrew scriptures, death was not seen as a separation of body and soul, as the Greeks perceived it. Death was described as a departure of breath (*ruach*) from the body (as in Psalm 104:29 and Job 12:10) or a pouring out of blood (Leviticus 17:11; Deuteronomy 12:23). The Christian scriptures describe death as a giving up of the Spirit (Matthew 27:50; Luke 23:46). Christianity teaches that in baptism we enter into Christ's death and resurrection and begin to live eternal life. Eucharist is an ongoing experience of death to self and rebirth into union with God. In our nightly prayers we entrust our lives to God, our nightly sleep being a symbol of death. These ongoing experiences prepare us to embrace death, as Cardinal Bernardin so recently did, as a friend. For a Christian, death is part of the great mystery, ushering us into union with God.

It is in our nature to seek God because we were created to live eternally in union with God. Jesus prayed "that they may be one...as we are one" (John 17:22). To be united with God, therefore, is to enter into communion with others. These two beliefs, that we are called to live eternally in union with God, and that to be united with God means to be in communion with humankind, are at the heart of Christian traditions of death and mourning.

How do we pass these beliefs on to our children? If the Christian belief about death is that death brings us into union with God and into communion with the saints, then children need to be included in our traditions of mourning. They need to experience the gathering together of Christians at the time of death, so that they can experience communion and union. If they are ignored at this time or excluded from these traditions, they are likely to grow up believing that death is about exclusion and separation.

Christian traditions of death and mourning come from the accumulated wisdom of centuries of faith in the face of human grief. They reflect what those who have gone before us understood about the needs of the dying and the bereaved. Traditions of final reconciliation and Communion and the gathering of loved ones about the deathbed address the dying person's need for healing and fellowship. Wakes and funeral traditions that celebrate the life of the deceased express Christian faith in eternal life. Vigils, funeral rites and ceremonies of closure, memorial meals, periods of mourning, visiting the bereaved and the observance of anniversaries all speak to the needs of those who grieve. Traditional prayers for the dead are a natural extension of our belief in eternal life and in the communion of saints.

Unfortunately, contemporary society is often at odds with these traditions. It can be difficult, for instance, to take the time off from work necessary to observe traditional periods of mourning that would help meet our emotional and spiritual needs. The breakup of extended families can mean that close family and friends will be unable to attend services or to visit and comfort one another. Hospitals may not provide the opportunity for large groups of families and friends to be with the dying person or to view the body. Often the body must be taken to the morgue within an hour after death, interfering with extended vigils. When faced with the death of a loved one, it is easier to go along with society rather than assert our beliefs and needs. Sometimes we will need to be outspoken, even in times of greatest weakness, so that we can come together to participate in healing traditions. At other times we will need to adapt traditions to fit contemporary life.

Traditions for the Dying

Oils have long been associated with healing. In fact, in Jesus' story the Good Samaritan anointed the man who had been robbed and beaten with oil (Luke 10:29-37). It has long been the practice in the Greek Orthodox community to receive this sacrament of Holy Unction once a year on Holy Wednesday of Holy Week, and privately as needed.[5] Among Catholics, the ancient practice of anointing the sick became associated with the dying; but since Vatican II, this sacrament is once again offered to anyone in need of healing.

There are many traditions of prayer meetings and vigils. Families gather together to pray when a person is critically ill or dying. Many families recite the rosary. In the Protestant tradition in which I was raised, it was common for family, friends and church members to call the prayer tree and keep a prayer vigil when someone was critically ill or dying.

Prayer Tree

Set up a prayer tree among your family and friends before it is needed. Talk to those family members or close friends who are willing to pray faithfully for serious concerns. Make a list with phone numbers, photocopy it and distribute to each participant. Then, instead of needing to call everyone, or worrying about whether someone was contacted in a critical situation, you can simply call the first person on the list, who calls the next person, who calls the next, and so on. Medical updates, answers to prayer, further information can all be communicated quickly and efficiently with one call.

It is customary among most Christians for family and friends to gather around the dying person, providing comfort through their presence. This is a sacred time. In my work as a chaplain, I have been privileged to share many such vigils. I have been deeply touched by families who are able to speak openly with each other at this time, assuring one another of their continued love, recalling poignant and humorous moments they have shared together. Often this is a time for reconciliation between family members, a time to heal long-inflamed familial wounds.

The deathbed confession is an ancient tradition that provides the dying person with an opportunity to reflect on his or her life, to confess and receive assurance of forgiveness for any sins he or she may have committed. In Jewish tradition, a critically ill person recites a prayer of confession called *Viddui*. In Christian tradition, a dying person celebrates the sacrament of reconciliation, or confession.

It is also traditional for the dying person to receive Communion (Viaticum). It can be a wonderful experience for family and friends to receive Communion with the dying person. It is an ancient tradition for the dying person to bless his or her loved ones at this time. Sometimes family members will wish to give the dying person their blessing. These blessings can be simple prayers in one's own words or familiar prayers of blessing. When giving a blessing you can make the sign of the cross on the forehead, recalling baptism, or place both hands on the person's head. When praying with the dying, you may wish to use familiar prayers, such as the Our Father and Hail Mary, or other prayers from scripture. Or you may wish to pray in your own words, voicing the thoughts and feelings in your heart, and inviting your loved ones to do the same.

Scriptural Prayers of Blessing in Difficult Times

- "Even though I walk through the darkest valley, I fear no evil; for you are with me." (Psalm 23:4)
- "Into your hand I commit my spirit." (Psalm 31:5)
- "For I am convinced that neither death, nor life, nor angels, nor rulers, nor things present, nor things to come, nor powers, nor height, nor depth, nor anything else in all creation, will be able to separate us from the love of God in Christ Jesus our Lord." (Romans 8:38-39)
- "When this perishable body puts on imperishability, and this mortal body puts on immortality, then the saying that is written will be fulfilled: 'Death has been swallowed up in victory.'" (1 Corinthians 15:54)
- "So we do not lose heart. Even though our outer nature is wasting away, our inner nature is being renewed day by day." (2 Corinthians 4:16)
- "For we know that if the earthly tent we live in is destroyed, we have a building from God, a house not made with hands, eternal in the heavens." (2 Corinthians 5:1)
- "We will be with the Lord forever." (1 Thessalonians 4:17)
- "See, the home of God is among mortals...God will wipe every tear from their eyes. Death will be no more; mourning and crying and pain will be no more." (Revelation 21:3-4)

It is a Jewish tradition to prepare an ethical will (*tzavaah*) for the family, especially for your children. What more important gift can you bequeath than your deepest beliefs, most central values, highest hopes? (Consult Israel Abraham's *Hebrew Ethical Wills*, 2 vols. [Philadelphia: Jewish Publication Society, 1976].) This tradition finds its root in Genesis 18:19 where God says of Abraham: "I have chosen him, that he may charge his children and his household after him to keep the way of the Lord by doing righteousness and justice." Ethical wills are a powerful way to pass the wisdom of one's life onto one's children. Generally, one makes an ethical will while still in good health, to be read by one's descendants after death.[6]

Traditions Following Death

From a therapist's perspective, one of the most important traditions following death is the viewing of the body. Initial denial is a normal human reaction to death, but people need ways to move gradually out of this denial, to take in the reality of their loss. Viewing the body can be extremely helpful in this process. Children should not be excluded. Gathering around the body, touching the body with respect and affection, honoring the body, sharing words of comfort and memories of the deceased, helps the mourners to acknowledge the reality of death, while finding comfort in the fellowship of one another.

In the Greek Orthodox tradition, the Trisagion service is said over the deceased at the time of death. It may be repeated in church or at the grave side on the third day, the ninth day, the fortieth day, at six months, one year and as needed throughout the first year.[7]

Vigils are another important tradition in most cultures. Often Christians who share a devotion to Mary pray the rosary together the evening before the funeral in the funeral home or church. The *veluda* is a candlelight watch from Hispanic tradition. Friends and family often come to spend the night. It is a Mexican tradition to say a novena, saying the rosary each night for a nine-day period after death.

Among the Vietnamese, it is traditional to keep the body in the home for three days. During this time the casket is open for viewing and the rosary is prayed repeatedly. In the United States, this tradition is often adapted and a vigil is kept at the church or funeral home. There is an African American tradition once called "sit-ups," when family and close friends gather together in the home of the immediate family to keep vigil. The immediate family is not expected to cook, so food and beverages are provided by friends to serve the numerous visitors who call to pay their condolences. "Sit-ups" are not practiced as often nowadays but have been replaced by wakes on the evening before the funeral.[8] It is customary among

African Americans in the southeastern states to place a wreath on the door of the family's home and leave the front porch light burning until the end of the funeral.[9] In Greece many mourners keep a 24-hour vigil beside the body; in the United States it is more common for the viewing of the body to take place for several hours at the funeral home.[10]

The primary ceremony of closure is the funeral or memorial service held in the church, followed by a service of prayers at the grave side. In the Christian tradition, the primary symbols used in the funeral rite are holy water (recalling baptism), the Easter candle (a sign of Christ's presence), the white cloth, called a pall, (covering the coffin as a sign of baptism), and the Bible or Book of the Gospels (placed on the coffin as a sign of faithfulness to God's word). In one Greek tradition, the pall used at death is the same white sheet used to receive the child at baptism.

Since the 13th century in Western tradition, black was associated with mourning. In other Christian traditions white, the color of resurrection, is more likely to be used. The clothing in which the deceased is buried can have great significance. Members of religious orders, including third orders, are often clothed in their habit. Sometimes the deceased is clothed in his or her wedding garments or in white, recalling baptism. Sometimes the deceased wears a crucifix, cross or scapular. In Greek tradition, a paper icon may be placed over the deceased's heart.[11] It is customary in many traditions to place flowers on the coffin, or to throw a handful of dirt on the coffin, recalling the scripture: "Dust you are and to dust you shall return" (Genesis 3:19).

Wakes and Memorial Meals

Following the funeral rites, many families serve food during vigils, wakes and memorial meals. Wakes, traditional in Polish and Irish communities, are parties that celebrate the life of the deceased. They provide mourners with an opportunity to gather together, tell stories and share memories. This can be a time for tears, but is as likely to be a time for laughter, a time when remembered joys begin to heal the pain of loss and the presence of loved ones makes more real the promise of eternal communion.

Storytelling and humor are an important part of the healing process. In Filipino tradition, everyone gathers in the house after the burial, and they begin to observe nine days of prayer. On the fortieth day, family and friends gather for a big party, celebrating the life of the deceased. It is a Mexican custom for each person to ask the mourner to tell the story of how the death occurred. As the story is told and retold, the shock lessens, the reality of loss sinks in, and gradually, one begins to pick up one's life and live on.[12] In Greek Orthodox tradition, the *makaria*, a somber meal, follows the funeral service. It may be shared in the home, church hall or at a restaurant. Often brandy, coffee and a dry anise-flavored bread called *praximathia* are served at this meal.[13] In many cultures families serve fish, a symbol of Christianity, at the memorial meal. In Jamaican tradition, the initial mourning period of nine days and nights is devoted to remembrance and storytelling. A meal of fried fish symbolizes Christ's feeding of fish to the multitude.[14]

Traditions of Remembrance

The many traditions of remembrance help mourners make the difficult adjustment from life with the loved one to life without him or her. In many cultures, mourners wear different clothing during the periods of mourning. Dark or black clothing is often worn to the funeral and may be worn for a period of time following. Sometimes a black ribbon or armband is worn. Filipina women often wear black and Filipino men wear a black ribbon on their shirt for an entire year following the death of a family member. Vietnamese mourners may wear funeral garments with a hood attached. Greeks traditionally wear dark clothes during the first forty days, sometimes combining black with white to indicate both death and resurrection. It used to be traditional to wear the wedding band of one's deceased spouse on your ring finger, both in remembrance and as a symbol of faith in the eternal union of Christian marriage. Black banners may be hung at the front of the house or black cloth draped over the doorway.

Most traditions mark periods of intensive and less intensive mourning. In the Jewish tradition the first seven days following the funeral is a period of intense mourning, called *shiva*. There is also a thirty-day mourning period and the *yahrzeit*, the one-year anniversary marked by prayer, the lighting of a candle and the recitation of the *Kaddish* prayer. In the early Christian church, it was customary to remember the dead on the third, seventh and thirtieth days.

Many Christian traditions, as already stated, observe a three-day, a nine-day and forty-day mourning period as well as a one-year anniversary. Families may attend church together on these days, enjoy family meals or visit the graves of the deceased. The three-day mourning reminds us that Christ lay in the tomb three days. The nine-day period affirms the belief that the deceased has joined the nine choirs of angels. The forty days recalls both the wandering in the desert after the exodus and the forty days of Jesus' temptation. In the Greek tradition, a dish called *Kollyva*, made from boiled wheat, sugar and spices, is served at the forty-day memorial. The dish symbolizes that we, like wheat, must be buried in order to grow into new life.[15]

After the intensive mourning has passed and we begin to settle back into daily routines, grief hits us anew. We may feel lost in the desert of our grief at this time, and it can help to call to mind how God continues to lead those who trust in him, out of the desert of loss and temptation, into a promised land of freedom and communion. There is a lovely tradition among Native American Christians in which the family has a party on the one-year anniversary following death. Close family and friends who attended the funeral and supported the family through their mourning are given gifts by the family as a thank-you for their support.

In 998, the Benedictine monastery at Cluny began celebrating a feast to remember the dead on November 2. By the 13th century, this practice was so widespread that Rome placed the feast day on the universal church calendar. It became customary to remember the saints in heaven on November 1 (All Saints) and those in purgatory on November 2 (All Souls).[16] In Hispanic tradition, All Saints (called the Day of the Dead) is elaborately celebrated with candies and toys in the shape of skeletons, coffins and skulls. A traditional holiday bread called *pan de los muertos* is served.[17]

In honoring and remembering the dead on anniversaries and All Souls, many Catholics celebrate Mass with family and friends of the deceased and visit the graves. It is an ancient custom in many cultures to visit the graves of the deceased, saying prayers there. Often people care for the graves at this time, decorating the graves with flowers or with blankets of evergreens (symbol of immortality).[18]

Filipino families gather at the cemetery after Mass on All Saints. They light candles, pray the rosary and bring food to share. Vietnamese families traditionally visit graves on November 1 or on Sundays. They clean the grave site, decorate it with a wreath and invite the souls of the deceased to come home for Lunar New Year. Vietnamese Americans often have ancestral altars in their homes where they offer flowers and fruit and burn incense. In this way they honor the deceased, keep alive cherished memories, and express their faith in the eternal communion of souls who live in Christ.

Another traditional way of remembering the deceased is by giving to the poor. This is an old Jewish tradition of *tzedakah* that has become traditional among Christians. Sometimes families ask that memorial gifts be made to a charity rather than having flowers sent. Sometimes a family member makes a donation in memory of the deceased to a charity or to their house of worship.

Sustaining Traditions of the Heart

Sometimes traditions from the past are not enough and people look for personal ways of remembering their loved ones and processing their grief. People I have worked with have kept a photo of the deceased and lit a candle by it on important anniversaries and holidays. One woman, whose husband loved to garden, planted his favorite flowers outside her bedroom window. Another wrote a brief letter to her loved one, attached it to a large leaf and let it float down a river. You might also attach words of love and remembrance to a feather or balloon. You might obtain a recording of a loved one's favorite song and play it on special days or go on a picnic or to a place you enjoyed together. Often we avoid memories and feelings because they are painful. Traditions of mourning encourage us to face the pain and to integrate our memories into our daily life. In time, our loved ones live on in our memories, calling us to a deeper and more authentic faith in the promises of Christ.

When my mother-in-law was dying of cancer at home with her family gathered about her, I remember the joy she took in playing with our new baby, Elizabeth. A life beginning and a life ending, finding joy in one another. The cycle of life is a never-ending circle of beginnings and endings, dyings and risings. In our dyings we need to remember the risings. In our rising we recall the dying. And we must celebrate it all, the joy and the pain, the receiving and the losing. We celebrate it all; for it is not a moment we celebrate, nor an event, nor an accomplishment. We celebrate life in its entirety. We celebrate the fullness, the richness, the mystery, the blessing of life.

Conclusion

The idea for this book came to me at a point of transition in my own family's life. We had moved from San Francisco to Chicago because of my husband's work. Country girl that I am, I suddenly found myself in a tiny temporary apartment in a high-rise overlooking not the ocean, but a lake, surrounded not by hills but by seemingly endless stretches of flat land, watching not the fog but snow creep over the landscape. I stood there thinking about friends and family who were far away. We had new addresses, new phone numbers, new winter clothes, new faces to meet, new schools and jobs, new places to worship and shop. The change in our lives was exciting but challenging and exhausting.

I knew that some families fall apart when faced with change and others grow stronger and healthier. What did my family need? My experience with my own family as well as with the families I've worked with over the years has taught me that the ability to draw on spiritual resources makes the difference. Spiritual traditions help us to live with an awareness of life's meaning and with an experience of communion. How easy it would have been, with the Advent wreath still in a box somewhere, to do without it this year. When the family meal involved coordinating schedules, shopping at unfamiliar stores and cooking in a kitchen too small for our things, fast food on the couch in front of the television had its appeal. Did it really matter if we said grace and sat down to eat together? Yet I knew that our family traditions were the concrete way in which we nourished our family life. I knew that we needed these simple traditions now more than ever. And if I forgot, my children and my husband, God bless them, were quick to remind me.

Our society is in transition. Families are dealing with high levels of stress and change and many of us are tempted, as I was tempted, to abandon the traditions of the past as inconvenient, time-consuming or irrelevant. We simply cannot afford to give in to this temptation. Those who never grew up with spiritual traditions may find it difficult at first to borrow from others or create their own, but it is important; no, more than that, it is vital that we do so. We must give as much thought and care to nourishing our children's spirits as we give to nourishing their bodies.

I remember hunting for my Easter baskets when I was a child. I would find my Easter goodies obviously protruding from behind the curtain or peeking out from under a stuffed animal. Why had it taken me so long to see them? It was easy for my sleepy parents to hide things in my room because my room was always so cluttered. As I worked on this book I continually felt I was unearthing buried treasure: a wealth of wonderful ways to experience God in family life. As in my childhood, most of these treasures were "buried" in plain sight: in the experience of friends, family and neighbors, in books at my local library, in my own memory and imagination. When our lives are cluttered with a zillion things demanding our attention, it is easy to overlook the signs of God's presence lovingly "hidden" before our eyes.

This book is not a definitive encyclopedia of Christian traditions. It is an invitation to search for God's presence in the daily stuff of life: planting a garden, cooking a meal, nursing an infant, visiting Grandma. I hope you have found some traditions here that will enrich your own family life. More importantly, I hope I have whetted your appetite and encouraged you to explore for yourself our rich spiritual heritage. I pray that God may bless your family with joy, love, a spirit of thanksgiving and a deep, abiding peace.

Endnotes

Introduction: TRADITIONS FOR LIVING

1. John P. Donnelly, ed., *Prayers and Devotions from Pope John XXIII* (New York: Image Books, 1969), 63.

Chapter 1: SANCTIFYING SOLITUDE

1. Susan Muto, *Celebrating the Single Life* (New York: Doubleday, 1982), 9.
2. Salvador Minuchin, *Families and Family Therapy* (Cambridge, MA: Harvard University Press, 1974), 47.
3. Muto, 41.
4. Anthony de Mello, *Saddhana* (New York: Doubleday, 1978), 37.
5. Bishop's Committee on the Liturgy, *Catholic Household Blessings and Prayers* (Collegeville, MN: Liturgical Press, 1988), 374.
6. Martin Buber, *I and Thou* (New York: Charles Scribner's Sons, 1958), 33, 11.

Chapter 2: FROM DATING TO COURTSHIP

1. Ellen K. Rothman, *Hands and Hearts: A History of Courtship in America* (New York: Basic Books, 1984), 102.
2. Rothman, 161.
3. Rothman, 164.
4. Cheryl Mercer, *Honorable Intentions, The Manner of Courtship in the 80s* (New York: Atheneum, 1983), 21.
5. H. Kirschenbaum and R. Stensrud, *The Wedding Book: Alternative Ways to Celebrate Marriage* (New York: Ballantine Books, 1984), 213.
6. Ethel Urlin, *A Short History of Marriage* (Detroit: Singing Tree Press), 230.
7. Urlin, 87.

Chapter 3: MATRIMONY AND MARRIAGE

1. Anthony Kosnik, Chairperson, *Human Sexuality* (New York: Paulist Press, 1977), 37.
2. W. Kaspar, *Theology of Christian Marriage* (New York: Seabury Press, 1980), 33.
3. S. Dahl, *Modern Bride's Guide to Your Wedding* (New York: Ballantine Press, 1984) 154.
4. Urlin, 62, 71, 111.
5. Patricia Williams, "The Cap, the Veil and the Apron," *Gwiazda Polarna* (May 1995), 6-9.
6. Paul Tillich, *The New Being* (New York: Charles Scribner Sons, 1955), 46.
7. Kirschenbaum and Stensrud, 232.

8. Urlin, 233.

9. Greg Dues, *Catholic Customs and Traditions: A Popular Guide* (Mystic, CT: Twenty-Third Publications, 1993), 168.

10. Herbert G. Gutman, *The Black Family in Slavery and Freedom* (New York: Pantheon Books) 273-282.

Chapter 4: IN THE BEGINNING

1. J.H. Hertz, ed., *The Pentateuch and Haflorahs*, *2nd ed.*, (London: Soncino Press, 1980), 2.

2. Barbara Katz Rothman, *Encyclopedia of Childbearing* (Phoenix, AZ: Oryx Press, 1993), 70-71.

3. Sheila Kitzinger, *Ourselves as Mothers* (Reading, MA: Addison-Wesley Publishing Co., 1995), 75.

4. Kitzinger, 20, 79.

5. Margaret Mead and Ken Heyman, *Family* (New York: McMillan, 1965), 15.

6. Kitzinger, 14.

7. Thomas Verny and Pamela Weintraub, *Nurturing the Unborn Child* (New York: Delacorte Press, 1991), xix.

8. *Catholic Household Blessings and Prayers*, 217 ff.

9. Kitzinger, 75.

10. Verny and Weintraub.

11. Mircea Eliade, ed., *The Encyclopedia of Religion* (New York: Macmillan and Co., 1987), 230.

12. *Encyclopedia Judaica*, Vol. 4 (New York: Macmillan Co., 1971), 1049-1053.

13. Rothman, 69-70.

14. Chloe Sayer, *Crafts of Mexico* (New York: Doubleday, 1977), 80, 109.

15. St. Basil, *Adv. Eunomium III*, 1: PG 29, 656 B, in *Catechism of the Catholic Church* (New York: Doubleday, 1995), 98.

16. Talmud B, Giffin 57a.

17. (Midrash, Eccleciastes Rabbah, 7:1), quoted in Sharon Strassfeld and Kathy Green, *The Jewish Family Book* (New York: Bantam Books, 1981), 20.

18. Simeon Maslin, ed., *Gates of Mitzah: A Guide to the Jewish Life Cycle* (New York: Central Conference of American Rabbis, 1979), 71.

19. Francis Weisser, *Handbook of Christian Feasts and Customs* (New York: Harcourt, Brace and Jovanovich, 1958), 181.

20. Marilyn Rouvelas, *A Guide to Greek Traditions and Customs in America* (Bethesda, MD: Attica Press, 1993), 85.

21. Rouvelas, 38-39.

22. Jan Riordan, *A Practical Guide to Breastfeeding* (Boston, MA: Jones and Bartlett Publishers, 1991), 4-7.

23. Riordan, 298-301.
24. Riordan, 302.
25. Riordan, 304.
26. *Catechism of the Catholic Church*, 343.
27. *Catechism of the Catholic Church*, 114.
28. Rouvelas, 33.
29. *Catechism of the Catholic Church*, 351.
30. Rouvelas, 165-166.
31. Rouvelas, 33.
32. *Catechism of the Catholic Church*, 349.
33. Rouvelas, 42.
34. F. R. Webber, *Church Symbolism* (Cleveland: J. H. Jansen, 1938), 74-75.
35. Rouvelas, 36.
36. Evelyn Birge Vitz, *A Continual Feast* (San Francisco: Ignatius Press, 1985), 26.
37. Rouvelas, 40.

Chapter 5: RITUALS AND RHYTHMS
1. Peter Farb and George Armelagos, *Consuming Passions: The Anthropology of Eating* (Boston: Houghton Mifflin, 1980), 212-13.
2. Vitz, 50.
3. Farb and Armelagos, 204.
4. Margaret Visser, *Much Depends on Dinner* (New York: Grove Press, 1986), 33.
5. John Brook, *The School of Prayer: An Introduction to the Divine Office for All Christians* (Collegeville, MN: Liturgical Press, 1990), 30.
6. Brook, 32.
7. *Catholic Household Blessings and Prayers*, 363-364.
8. Hennig Cohen and Tristram Potter Coffin, eds., *The Folklore of American Holidays* (Detroit, MI: Gale Research Co., 1987), 113-114.
9. Maslin, 85.
10. Rouvelas, 160.
11. Hubert Van Zeller, *The Holy Rule* (Kansas City, MO: Sheed and Ward, 1958), 330.
12. Maslin, 121-122.
13. Adin Steinsaltz, *Teshuvah* (New York: The Free Press, 1982), 140.

Chapter 6: MARKING THE YEARS
1. Rouvelas, 97.
2. Weisser, 280.
3. Vitz, 24-25.

4. Katherine Kirlin, *Smithsonian Folklore Cookbook* (Washington, D.C.: Smithsonian Institution Press, 1992), 184.

5. Rouvelas, 96-97.

6. Weisser, 282.

7. Morris Bishop, *The Horizon Book of Middle Ages* (New York: American Heritage Publishing Co., 1968), 132.

8. Rouvelas, 226-227.

9. Maslin, 32.

10. Dues, 23.

11. Dues, 22.

12. Dues, 26-28.

13. Cohen and Coffin, 363.

14. Weisser, 225-226.

15. Weisser, 294-295.

16. Lesley Bremness, *Herbs* (New York: Dorling Kindersley, 1994), 159, 223.

17. Henry Bestow, *Herbs and the Earth* (Boston: David R. Gretine, 1990), 56.

18. Adelma Grenier Simmons, *A Merry Christmas Herbal* (New York: William Morrow and Co., 1968), 96-97, 127-128.

19. *Carmelite Devotions* (Milwaukee, WI: The Bruce Publishing Co., 1956), 143.

20. Cohen and Coffin, 257-258.

21. Cohen and Coffin, 69, 132.

Chapter 7: LOVING THE ADOLESCENT

1. Erik Erikson, *Childhood and Society*, 2nd ed., (New York: W.W. Norton and Co., 1963), 150.

2. James P. Lyke, OFM, Auxiliary Bishop of Cleveland, *Say Not "I am too Young,"* a Pastoral Reflection addressed to African American youth of the Archdiocese of Cleveland, Ohio, 1990 and A. J. McKnight, C.S., "A Black Christian Perspective of Spirituality: *Theology: A Portrait in Black*, no. 1, ed. by Thaddeus J. Posey, OFM, 1980, 110.

3. Charles Smith, SVD, and Chester P. Smith, SVD, *Boyhood to Manhood* (Techny, IL: Divine Word, 1993), 3-9.

4. Dues, 155.

5. *Catechism of the Catholic Church*, 365.

6. *Catechism of the Catholic Church*, 366-367.

7. Kirlin, 256.

Chapter 8: AGING AND DYING

1. Dues, 67.
2. For prayers to say when sharing Communion with the elderly see Bishop's Committee on the Liturgy edition of *Catholic Household Blessings and Prayers* (Collegeville, MN: Liturgical Press, 1988), 256-260.
3. Helen Caswell, *Shadows from the Singing House* (Tokyo, Japan: Charles E. Tuttle Co.,1968), 11-12.
4. As quoted in Sharon Strassfeld and Kathy Green's book, *The Jewish Family Book* (New York: Bantam Books, 1981), 380.
5. Rouvelas, 71.
6. Maslin, 51.
7. Rouvelas, 140-141.
8. Lynn Ann De Spelder and Alvert Lee Strickland, *The Path Ahead: Readings in Death and Dying* (Mountain View, CA: Mayfield Publishing Co, 1995), 89.
9. De Spelder and Strickland, 88.
10. Rouvelas, 140.
11. Rouvelas, 140-141.
12. Deborah Duda, *A Guide to Dying At Home* (Santa Fe, NM: John Muir Publishing, 1982), 244.
13. Rouvelas, 142.
14. Evan Imber-Black, *Rituals for our Times* (New York: HarperCollins Publishing, 1987), 271.
15. Rouvelas, 144-145.
16. Dues, 135.
17. Earl Grollman, *Bereaved Children and Teens* (Boston: Beacon Press, 1995), 82.
18. Dues, 138.